The Financial Buddha

Vridham

Contents

Preface

In a society that frequently disregards financial literacy, it is crucial to understand money and investing. Building a safe and prosperous future requires having the right instruments and tactics as we traverse an ever-more complicated financial world. The idea behind this book was to make difficult financial ideas easier to understand so that readers could make wise financial decisions.

My path has been everything but typical over the years. Even though I've worked in the Indian film industry for a large portion of my career, my passion for finance has really influenced both my professional and personal development. I put my expertise into practice after personally witnessing the benefits of prudent financial planning. I have been actively implementing Greek-based trading strategies in the Indian financial markets for the past seven years, developing a comprehensive understanding of the complexities and dynamics that contribute to success. However, this book will not cover the complicated nature of Greek-based strategies, as they require significant expertise and direct interaction with the live market. Such sophisticated methods are best left to experienced traders and are outside the purview of this book.

I would like to present a new approach to finance in this book, one that strikes a balance between conventional wisdom and cutting-edge tactics. You will discover useful guidance on risk management, asset allocation, and investing tactics that are appropriate for people at various phases of their financial development. This book is intended to help you manage the complexity of confidently managing your finances, from debunking myths about real estate investing to exposing the nuances of the stock market.

Regardless of your level of experience, I hope that the information presented here will motivate you to take charge of your financial destiny and make choices that support your objectives.

Together, let's go out on this road for progress, financial independence, and clarity on your route to wealth accumulation.

Enjoy your reading!

Chapter 1

What is Wealth?

As I embark on this trip to explore the concept of wealth, I am reminded of the rich tapestry of Indian culture, where ideas of prosperity and abundance are deeply embedded. But what exactly does wealth signify in the context of our lives? Join me as we explore the riddles of wealth and its importance in Indian culture.

In India, prosperity goes well beyond tangible belongings. It entails a comprehensive sense of wealth that includes not just material prosperity but also spiritual, emotional, and familial well-being. Our ancient traditions, such as the Vedas and Upanishads, include significant insights regarding the varied nature of wealth.

"Artha," one of the four Purusharthas (life's aims), refers to the desire for material wealth and prosperity. It is a core concept in Indian philosophy. However, Artha involves more than merely acquiring wealth; it also involves using one's possessions properly for the benefit of oneself and others. Affluence and the concept of "Karma" (action) are strongly linked in Indian philosophy. The idea that our deeds, whether good or negative, influence our fate and financial success is essential to the belief in karma. That is why our goals and actions have a greater impact on our wealth than do external factors.

Furthermore, in its pursuit of prosperity, Indian culture stresses the significance of connections and communal bonds. The idea of "Sambandha" shows how people are related to one another in society and how important support systems and social networks are for success.

Money, or "Dharma" in Hinduism, is seen as a tool to achieve a greater good. Affluence paves the door to responsibility and obligation fulfilment in many forms, including but not limited to providing for one's family, giving to worthy organizations, and improving one's community. Having a lot of money isn't the only definition of wealth in Hinduism; a strong sense of contentment, harmony, and general health are all part of it. The trick is to strike a balance between achieving personal success and achieving social good; between pursuing financial wealth and achieving spiritual enlightenment.

Let us, then, as we explore the meaning of wealth more thoroughly, strive not simply to accumulate material possessions but also to develop the kind of interior riches—the wealth of wisdom, compassion, and virtues—that defines our individual and collective prosperity. Come along with me as we explore the profound meaning of wealth in Indian philosophy.

Defining Wealth:

Luxury is sometimes mistaken for monetary success and material goods in the fast-paced world in which we live. As we explore more of the topic, though, we realize that true wealth encompasses a great deal more than simply monetary holdings. As part of it, we must take care of our physical health, establish real relationships with other people, and learn to enjoy the simple things in life.

Traditional wealth in Indian culture includes material success as well as emotional, intellectual, and spiritual well-being. The effect we have on other people, the happiness we experience when our deeds are in line with our values, and the quality of our relationships are more important than material wealth. Happiness and security brought about by worldly wealth are fleeting and cannot last. In contrast, a state of optimal health is an invaluable asset since it permits us to relish each moment with limitless energy and enthusiasm. Furthermore, having a vast network of loved ones who will continually support us is crucial, regardless of the circumstances.

It is not one's financial holdings but one's influence and the things one has achieved over their career that constitute real wealth. Spiritual wealth is highly prized in Indian culture because it leads to a more profound comprehension of the universe and our role in it.

With all our focus on getting money, let us not forget what it means to truly be rich. Engage in activities that promote well-being, such as reflection, thankfulness, and meditation; work on our relationships; and develop our inner strengths. Doing this will allow us to accumulate immeasurable wealth, as well as an eternal source of joy and contentment, regardless of the cost.

Types of Wealth:

From the shimmering gold that decorates our temples to the knowledge that has been handed down through the ages, wealth is seen in many forms throughout India. Preserving and valuing our cultural history is equally as important as accumulating wealth.

Let us revel in the variety of assets that contribute to the well-being of our communities and ourselves as we explore the various aspects of wealth. Our wealth lies not in the money accounts or the balance sheets of corporations, but in the rich fabric of our spirituality, traditions, languages, and arts.

Our old temples are more than just pretty walls; the exquisite sculptures and carvings that decorate them are expressions of our respect for the sacred and our will to keep our heritage alive. Furthermore, the beautiful and meaningful classical dances, music, and literature that have flourished in India for thousands of years are invaluable treasures that provide joy and empathy to people all over the world.

Our ancestors' knowledge, as recorded in poems, epics, and philosophical treatises, is likewise a valuable resource for us. These ageless teachings provide priceless wisdom about life's meaning, the search for truth, and the meaning of existence itself.

However, the universal feeling of unity and interconnection that characterizes Indian civilization is perhaps our most precious asset. Family and community bonds are priceless resources that help us get through tough times, whether it's the solace of a family reunion, the delight of a town fair, or the power of a nation coming together as a nation in times of crisis. When considering the meaning of wealth, we must not overlook the intangibles that improve our lives. Let us revere our ancestors' wisdom, cherish and maintain our cultural legacy, and strengthen the ties that bind us together as a nation. Doing so will protect our wealth for future generations, making life better for everyone in India.

The Psychology of Wealth:

Our views and thoughts about money are heavily influenced by our cultural upbringing and society traditions. In India, where the concept of "savings for a rainy day" is deeply embedded in our communal psyche, simplicity and financial prudence are highly valued characteristics.

We must also handle the attraction of consumption and the pressure to meet societal norms. Rapid economic expansion and globalisation have marked an era of unprecedented materialism, in which the desire of wealth and possessions frequently takes precedence over other elements of life.

In this complex context, understanding the psychology of wealth is critical. It entails investigating our idea, attitudes, and behaviours toward money and possessions, as well as the underlying motivations that drive our financial decisions.

For many Indians, the fear of shortage and instability acquired from previous generations drives our approach to money management. Saving for the future, investing in assets such as gold and real estate, and emphasizing financial security are deeply rooted cultural norms that reflect our desire for stability and protection from unexpected problems.

However, the advent of consumer culture, as well as the impact of media and advertising, have promoted an instant gratification and visible consuming mindset. The pressure to meet cultural expectations and maintain a specific quality of living can result in overspending, debt accumulation, and financial hardship.

Navigating these battling messages requires a conscious effort to match our financial decisions with our values and goals. It includes developing financial knowledge, practicing mindfulness regarding spending patterns, and creating a healthy relationship with money based on moderation and balance.

Better decisions that enhance our happiness and well-being in the long run can be made when we are aware of the psychological motivations that impact our financial choices. Taking charge of one's financial situation, whether by making reasonable plans, putting experiences ahead of possessions, or getting advice from experts when needed, can bring about more happiness and peace in life.

Finally, wealth psychology is about building a mindset of plenty, thankfulness, and purpose that enriches all part of our life, rather than simply amassing wealth. By accepting these ideas, we may manage the difficulties of modern economics with knowledge and resilience, ensuring a better future for ourselves and future generations.

Cultivating Wealth:

In today's dynamic economy, the ability to be financially literate has never been more important. In addition to the country's several prospects to generate wealth, one may acquire anything from the essential effort of the basics of budgeting and saving to exploring business and investing. By obtaining knowledge and skills, we all have the ability to affect our fiscal futures. Making a budget, paying off debt, and saving can help you get there in the long run with financial security. Furthermore, in a country packed with innovators and entrepreneurs, there is plenty to make money from investing and commercial pursuits. Numerous alternatives exist for producing money and accumulating wealth; investing in real estate, investing in the stock market, or launching a small business.

A mindset based on a lot, resilience, and adaptability is just as important as getting hold of money when it comes to developing wealth. To be ahead of the curve and grab opportunities when they come in today's ever-changing economic climate, it is essential to be open to learning and embrace change.

Moreover, building money is about more than just being successful; it's also about leaving a legacy of wealth to the generations who come after us.

Our children and grandchildren will have a higher chance of success in life if we take the time to strategically plan for their financial future now. Improving people's financial literacy and competence offers far-reaching personal advantages, while also being vital to the nation's overall economic advancement and development.

Economic stability, creativity, and prosperity are all enhanced when more individuals acquire the information and self-assurance to handle their money well. In order to achieve financial success, it is important to approach wealth accumulation with commitment, discipline, and a willingness to take calculated risks. With the right knowledge and mindset, we have the power to shape our financial future and create a lasting legacy of wealth that extends beyond our own lifetimes.

I am filled with hope and potential as we finish this chapter. In India, attaining financial success is considered a crucial component of a broader spiritual journey. We can discover the secret to wealth and live lives of richness and meaning when we commit to the principles of honesty, self-control, and charity.

Chapter 2

Mastering Financial Fundamentals

In this chapter, we will look into the core principles of financial literacy, providing a comprehensive guide to mastering the fundamentals of money management. From budgeting basics to debt management strategies and long-term financial planning, we will equip you with the knowledge and tools you need to take control of your financial future.

Basics of Budgeting:

Because it enables people to successfully manage their resources and work toward their financial goals, budgeting is the cornerstone of achieving financial stability.

Let us explore the complexity of budgeting and comprehend its importance by examining real-life examples:

Meet Ravi, a Bengaluru-based software engineer. Ravi's monthly income amounts to ₹50,000. He diligently monitors his earnings and expenditures to uphold financial oversight. Ravi initiates the process by classifying his earnings into primary sources, namely his salary, as well as supplementary sources such as freelance employment or rental revenue derived from his owned home.

Next, Ravi carefully keeps track of his expenses, categorizing them into fixed expenses like rent, utilities, insurance premiums, and variable costs like entertainment, eating out, and shopping.

Through a thorough analysis of his spending patterns, Ravi identifies opportunities to cut down on expenses, such as reducing the frequency of dining out or optimizing utility usage.

Ravi carefully analyses his income and expenses to create a monthly budget. He carefully manages his finances, making sure to prioritize his essential expenses such as rent, groceries, and utility bills. Ravi is diligent about saving and investing, ensuring that he allocates a portion of his income towards future objectives such as buying a house or securing his retirement. In addition, he sets aside a portion of his budget for non-essential expenses, but he is careful not to spend too much.

Ravi utilizes a range of tools, such as mobile apps and spreadsheets, to diligently track his expenses on a regular basis. He regularly reviews his budget, making necessary adjustments to account for any changes in income or expenses. With a keen eye for financial management, Ravi diligently sticks to his budget and steadily works towards his future goals, including owning a home and planning for retirement.

Similarly, let me present Priya, a marketing executive living in Mumbai. Priya makes a monthly salary of ₹40,000. Priya, like Ravi, uses a disciplined approach to budgeting to properly manage her funds.

Priya's budget includes both fixed expenses such as rent, utilities, and insurance fees, as well as variable expenses such as groceries, transportation, and discretionary spending like dining out and entertainment. She prioritizes savings and investments by setting aside a portion of her income to develop an emergency fund, contribute to a retirement savings account, and invest in mutual funds through SIPs.

To measure her progress toward financial goals, Priya sets precise goals, such as saving for a six-month emergency fund or saving for an annual vacation. She uses visual tools such as charts and graphs to track her financial progress and stays motivated to stick to her budget.

Ravi and Priya demonstrate the value of financial planning and responsible money management by implementing rigorous budgeting habits. Budgeting enables people to make informed financial decisions, prioritize their goals, and achieve financial stability and freedom.

Understanding Income and Expenses:

Income and expenses are the building blocks of our financial lives, shaping our ability to achieve our goals and aspirations. Let's delve deeper into how individuals can understand and manage their income and expenses effectively:

1. Sources of Income: Income can come from various sources, including:

- **Salary:** Regular income earned from employment.

- **Freelance Work:** Income earned from freelance or contract work.

- **Rental Income:** The revenue originates from the rental of assets or real estate.

- **Investment Income:** The money comes from investments, such as bond interest or stock dividends.

- **Side Businesses:** Income generated from side businesses or entrepreneurial ventures.

Understanding the different sources of income allows individuals to diversify their earnings and build multiple streams of income for financial stability.

2. Tracking Expenses: Expenses can be categorized into two main types:

- **Fixed Expenses:** These are typical monthly expenses that don't change much, such as utilities, insurance premiums, loan payments, rent or loan payments, and subscription services.

- **Variable Expenses:** These are the kinds of costs that can change from month to month: food, eating out, entertainment, travel, and extra money spent on things that aren't necessities.

- Those who closely monitor their expenses can gain valuable insights into their spending habits and identify areas for optimization or reduction.

3. Differentiating Between Needs and Wants: It's essential to distinguish between needs and wants when managing expenses:

- **Needs:** Essential expenses required for survival and maintaining a basic standard of living, such as food, shelter, utilities, and healthcare.

- **Wants:** Non-essential expenses that are desirable but not necessary for survival, such as dining out, entertainment, travel, and luxury items.

Prioritizing needs over wants ensures that individuals allocate their resources towards essential expenses first before indulging in discretionary spending.

4. Making a Budget: A budget is a financial plan that shows a person's anticipated income and outlays for a given time period, usually a month.

Making a budget involves:

- **Estimating Income:** Projecting expected income from all sources.

- **Listing Expenses:** Identifying all fixed and variable expenses.

- **Allocating Funds:** Assigning funds to various expense categories based on priority and importance.

- **Tracking Spending:** Monitoring actual spending against budgeted amounts and making adjustments as needed.

By adhering to a budget, individuals can manage their cash flow effectively, avoid overspending, and work towards their financial goals.

5. Managing Cash Flow: Cash flow management involves ensuring that there is enough money available to cover expenses and financial obligations as they arise. Strategies for managing cash flow include:

- **Creating an Emergency Fund:** Saving money for unforeseen costs or crises.

- **Timing Expenses:** Planning expenses to align with income receipt dates.

- **Avoiding Overdrafts or Late Payments:** Monitoring account balances to prevent overdrafts and ensuring timely payment of bills to avoid late fees.

By maintaining a positive cash flow and staying on top of expenses, individuals can avoid financial stress and maintain financial stability.

Debt Management Strategies:

Debt can be a significant obstacle to financial freedom, but with careful planning and discipline, it can be managed effectively. Here are some debt management strategies to consider:

1. Acknowledge Your Debt: Knowing what kind of debt you have is the first step towards controlling it.

- **Consumer Debt:** Debt incurred from purchasing consumer goods or services, such as credit card debt, personal loans, and installment loans.

- **Student Loans:** Debt taken out to finance higher education expenses.

- **Loans:** Debt associated with purchasing a home.

- **Car Loans:** Debt taken out to purchase a vehicle.

Having a thorough understanding of each debt's terms, interest rates, and repayment plans will help you create an efficient plan for managing and repaying your obligations.

2. Prioritize High-Interest Debt: Because interest accrues compound interest, high-interest debt, like credit card debt, can be especially taxing. Make extra payments on high-interest bills first, and only make the required minimum payments on other obligations in order to prioritize paying them off. This strategy can speed up debt repayment and lower interest expenses.

3. Consolidate Debt: A debt consolidation loan or a balance transfer credit card could help you to combine several debts into one loan with a reduced interest rate. Consolidating debt helps one to manage and pay off debt by simplifying repayment, lowering interest rates, and possibly decreasing monthly payments.

4. Negotiate with Creditors: If you find it difficult to pay your bills, don't hesitate to contact your creditors to go over other ways of repayment. Many creditors are willing to work with borrowers to modify repayment terms, such as reducing interest rates, extending loan terms, or temporarily suspending payments through forbearance or deferment programs.

5. Create a Repayment Plan: Create a payback schedule that shows how you will methodically address your debt. Consider implementing the debt snowball or debt avalanche method:

A. Debt Snowball Method:

The Debt Snowball Method emphasizes paying off the smallest debt first and making minimum payments on all other debts. Once you pay off the previous smallest debt, you apply the extra payment to the next smallest obligation.

This method provides psychological momentum by achieving quick wins. Here's how it works:

- **List Your Debts:** Regardless of interest rate, first list all of your loans from least to largest.

- **Pay Minimums:** Make minimum payments on all obligations except the smallest.

- **Attack the Smallest Debt:** Allocate any extra funds you have towards paying off the smallest debt. This could include additional income, cutting expenses, or reallocating funds from your budget.

- **Celebrate Quick Wins:** Celebrate your progress as you pay off each loan. Paying off a debt gives one a sense of success that can inspire one to keep on the intended course.

- **Roll Over Payments:** Once the smallest debt is paid off, take the amount you were paying towards it and apply it towards the next smallest debt. This "snowball effect" allows you to pay off debts quickly over time.

- **Repeat Until Debt-Free:** Continue this process until all your debts are paid off. With each debt you pay off, you'll have more money available to put towards the next one, accelerating your progress towards becoming debt-free.

The Debt Snowball Method works well because it emphasizes creating momentum and offering psychological incentives throughout. While it may not be the most cost-effective method in terms of minimizing interest payments, its simplicity and motivation factor make it a popular choice for many people striving to get out of debt.

B. Debt Avalanche Method:

The Debt Avalanche Method is a debt repayment strategy that focuses on paying off debts with the highest interest rates first while making minimum payments on all other debts. Once the highest-interest debt is paid off, you apply the extra payment towards the next highest-interest debt, and so on.

This method minimizes interest costs over time. Here's how it works:

- **List Your Debts:** Start by listing all your debts in order from highest to lowest interest rate.

- **Pay Minimums:** Make minimum payments on all your debts except the one with the highest interest rate.

- **Attack the Highest-Interest Debt:** Allocate any extra funds you have towards paying off the debt with the highest interest rate. This could include additional income, cutting expenses, or reallocating funds from your budget.

- **Reduce Interest Costs:** Concentrating on the debt with the highest interest rate helps you reduce the total interest paid over time, allowing you to save money.

- **Roll Over Payments:** Once the highest-interest debt is paid off, take the amount you were paying towards it and apply it towards the next highest-interest debt. This allows you to "avalanche" your payments towards becoming debt-free.

- **Repeat Until Debt-Free:** Continue this process until all your debts are paid off. As you eliminate each high-interest debt, you'll have more money available to put towards the next one, accelerating your progress towards financial freedom.

The Debt Avalanche Method works well because it makes paying off high-interest debt a top priority, saving you money on interest over time. Although it may take more time to observe improvement than the Debt Snowball Method, it eventually results in faster debt repayment and lower overall interest expenses.

6. Avoid Taking on New Debt: Try to pay off current debt; if possible, stay away from acquiring additional debt. Reduce discretionary spending, set a budget, and save an emergency fund to help with unanticipated costs without turning to debt. By living within your means and prioritizing debt repayment, you can break the cycle of debt and achieve financial freedom.

7. Seek Professional Help if Needed: See a qualified credit counsellor or financial advisor if debt overwhelms you or you find it difficult to create a payback schedule. These experts can offer you individualized advice and encouragement to enable you to properly handle your debt.

Chapter 3

Value of Money

This chapter will cover the idea of money's value as well as how to tell the difference between unnecessary spending and beneficial investments. Knowing the real value of the things we buy helps us make wise decisions that fit our priorities and financial goals.

1. Differentiating Between Needs and Wants:

Knowing the difference between needs and wants is essential before making any purchases. Desires are choices that improve our quality of life but are not necessary, whereas needs are necessities for survival and upholding a minimal standard of living. Setting needs above wants enables us to spend money wisely and utilize our resources more effectively.

Example:

Consider the decision to buy a new smartphone. While a smartphone is considered a requirement for communication and work-related duties, purchasing the most recent model with advanced capabilities may be more of a want than a need. Assessing if the extra features justify the increased price might help you decide whether the purchase is a worthy investment or an unnecessary spend.

In this case, the requirement for a smartphone for communication and work is constant regardless of model or features. However, upgrading to a newer model with greater capabilities is a choice rather than a requirement. By determining whether the additional features connect with your priorities and give concrete benefits, you can make an informed judgment about whether the purchase is justified or if it is better to prioritize other financial goals.

Individuals can make more responsible financial decisions by continually distinguishing between needs and wants, ensuring that their resources are directed to necessary spending and meaningful investments that match with their long-term goals and priorities.

2. Assessing Long-Term Value:

The long-term effects of a purchase must be taken into account while determining its worth. Will the item remain and offer benefits for a long time, or will it suddenly become outdated or lose its appeal? We can avoid impulsive purchases and instead make decisions that advance our long-term financial well-being by evaluating a purchase's long-term worth.

Example:

Consider choosing between a high-end laptop with premium features and a low-cost laptop. Even if the high-end laptop has more advanced features and greater performance, the price is significantly higher. To determine whether the purchase is a sound investment or an unnecessary indulgence, consider whether the new features outweigh the cost in terms of increased productivity or user pleasure.

In this situation, an affordable laptop may meet the requirements for basic computing equipment for both personal and professional use. It is a good choice for people with limited budgets or modest computing requirements because it offers minimal capabilities at a lower cost.

A high-end laptop with premium features, on the other hand, may have more advanced specifications, such as faster CPUs, better screens, and more storage. These features cost more than others, but they can boost productivity and make using the product more enjoyable.

Assessing whether the additional features justify the cost involves considering factors such as:

A. **Usage Requirements:** Evaluate your individual computing requirements and determine whether the additional capabilities of the high-end laptop are appropriate for your usage habits. If you need to conduct intense work like video editing, graphic design, or gaming, the high-end laptop's greater performance may be warranted.

B. **Long-Term Value:** Consider the investment's longevity and if the high-end laptop's advanced capabilities will remain useful and practical over time. Investing in a high-quality gadget with future-proof characteristics might provide value for several years, as opposed to a low-cost laptop, which may become obsolete sooner.

C. **Budget Constraints:** Assess your financial standing to see if the higher price of the high-end laptop is within your budget. While the advanced features may be appealing, it is critical to prioritize financial security and avoid overextending yourself financially.

By carefully analyzing the costs and benefits of each choice, you can make an informed selection that is appropriate for your requirements, preferences, and financial situation. Whether you choose a budget laptop that fulfills basic computing demands or a high-end laptop for improved performance and capabilities, understanding the value proposition of each option ensures that your resources are deployed properly to achieve your objectives.

3. Opportunity Cost:

Every purchase involves an opportunity cost—the value of the next best alternative forgone. By considering the opportunity cost of a purchase, we can evaluate whether the benefits outweigh the alternatives and make choices that maximize our overall satisfaction and utility.

Example:

Suppose you have the option to spend ₹50,000 on a weekend getaway or invest the same amount in a mutual fund for future financial growth. While the weekend getaway may offer immediate gratification and relaxation, investing in the mutual fund has the potential to generate long-term returns and financial security. Considering the opportunity cost allows you to weigh the benefits and trade-offs of each option and make a decision aligned with your priorities and values.

In this scenario, the weekend getaway represents a want rather than a need. It offers an opportunity for leisure and relaxation, providing a break from the routine of daily life. However, it involves a one-time expenditure with no lasting financial benefit.

On the other hand, investing ₹50,000 in a mutual fund offers the potential for significant long-term financial growth. Over time, the value of your investment can grow through capital appreciation and dividend payments, providing a source of passive income and financial security for the future.

By considering the opportunity cost, you can weigh the benefits and trade-offs of each option:

A. **Immediate Gratification vs. Long-Term Gain:** The weekend getaway provides immediate gratification and relaxation, while investing in the mutual fund offers the potential for substantial long-term financial growth and security.

B. **Short-Term Experience vs. Lasting Benefits:** The weekend getaway offers a short-term experience with memories that may fade over time, while investing in the mutual fund provides lasting benefits through the accumulation of wealth and financial stability.

C. **Personal Values and Priorities:** Consider your personal values and priorities when making the decision. If you prioritize experiences and quality time with loved ones, the weekend getaway may align better with your values. However, if you value financial security and long-term planning, investing in the mutual fund may be a more prudent choice.

Ultimately, the decision depends on your individual circumstances, goals, and values. By carefully weighing the opportunity cost and considering the long-term implications of each option, you can make a decision that aligns with your priorities and sets you on the path towards financial well-being.

Chapter 4

Managing Depreciating Assets: The Case of Car Ownership

In India, having a car is frequently regarded as a status, practicality, and mobility symbol. Cars are being considered depreciating assets in financial terms, which means their value decreases with time, and this must be understood. Knowing the benefits and drawbacks of owning a car in this situation, as well as how to save costs on depreciating assets like cars, is crucial.

Pros of Car Ownership:

1. **Convenience:** Having a car provides convenience and flexibility in transportation, allowing you to travel at your own pace and schedule without relying on public transport.

2. **Status Symbol:** In Indian society, owning a car is often associated with prestige and social status, especially in urban areas where car ownership is seen as a sign of success.

3. **Mobility:** A car offers greater mobility and accessibility, allowing you to explore new places, commute to work, and run errands with ease.

Cons of Car Ownership:

1. **Depreciation:** One of the biggest drawbacks of car ownership is depreciation. Cars lose value over time due to factors such as wear and tear, technological advancements, and market demand. This means that the resale value of your car decreases significantly, leading to financial loss.

2. **Maintenance Costs:** Cars require regular maintenance, including servicing, repairs, and fuel expenses. These costs can add up over time and contribute to the overall expense of car ownership.

3. **Insurance and Taxes:** Car owners are required to pay for insurance premiums and vehicle taxes, which can be significant expenses depending on the type and value of the car.

Saving Money on Car Ownership:

1. **Buy Used Cars:** Consider purchasing a used car instead of a brand new one. Since used cars have already seen the first depreciation, they are more reasonably priced choices. However, be sure to thoroughly inspect the vehicle's condition and history before making a purchase.

2. **Choose Fuel-Efficient Models:** Opt for cars with good fuel efficiency to save money on fuel

expenses in the long run. Hybrid or electric cars may also be viable options for reducing fuel costs and environmental impact.

3. **Limit Optional Features:** While fancy features and accessories may enhance the driving experience, they also increase the cost of the car. Consider opting for basic models with essential features to save money on upfront costs.

4. **Negotiate for Discounts:** Don't hesitate to negotiate with dealerships for discounts, promotions, or incentives when purchasing a car. Researching market prices and comparing offers from multiple sellers can help you secure the best deal.

5. **Invest in Maintenance:** Regular maintenance and servicing can prolong the lifespan of your car and reduce the likelihood of costly repairs in the future. Follow the manufacturer's recommended maintenance schedule and address any issues promptly to avoid larger expenses down the line.

Example:

As a responsible automobile owner, Rohan is aware of the financial ramifications of having a depreciating asset such as a car. Let's examine his financial journey, the benefits and drawbacks of car ownership, and methods for reducing depreciation losses.

Rohan's Financial Commitment:

After extensive research, Rohan decides on a ₹10,000,00 INR sedan that is both dependable and fuel-efficient. This is an account of his money:

1. **Car Purchase Price (Ex Showroom):** ₹10,00,000 INR

2. **Down Payment:** ₹2,00,000 INR

3. **Loan Amount:** ₹8,00,000 INR

Loan Details:

- **Interest Rate:** 8% per annum

- **Loan Term:** 7 years

Using the formula for calculating the total payment on a loan, Rohan calculates the total interest paid over the 7-year loan term to be ₹2,47,394 INR.

Total Cost of Ownership for Rohan over 7 years:

1. **Loan Amount:** ₹8,00,000 INR

2. **Road Tax:** ₹1,10,000 INR (As per Maharashtra's Road tax)

3. **Insurance Premium (7 years):** ₹1,05,000 (Approximate Values)

4. **GST on Insurance (7 years):** ₹18,900

5. **Maintenance:** ₹1,12,000 (Approximate Values)

6. **Down Payment:** ₹2,00,000

7. **Total Interest Paid on Loan:** ₹2,47,394

Total Money Spent by Rohan over 7 years: ₹15,93,294

This detailed breakdown provides insight into Rohan's financial commitment, including the down payment, loan interest, and total cost of ownership over the 7-year period.

Understanding Depreciation:

For car owners, depreciation—the slow, steady decrease in an asset's value over time—is an important factor. Even with careful upkeep, Rohan's car experiences significant depreciation; after 7 years, he only gets ₹4,00,000 INR when he sells it, barely making up for his original outlay.

In the end, even if having a car can be convenient and provide mobility, it's important to assess the financial costs and take into account other options like public transit, carpooling, or ridesharing services. Over time, you may reduce the cost of depreciating assets and manage the challenges of car ownership by emphasizing financial stability and making well-informed decisions.

Important Notice:

Please be aware that all of the data presented here are merely meant to serve as examples and might not precisely depict financial situations found in the real world. These numbers are not meant to be interpreted as financial advice or assistance; rather, they are meant to be used as examples to help clarify the concepts covered. Real financial decisions ought to be founded on unique situations, in-depth investigation, and advice from licensed financial experts.

Chapter 5

The Power of Credit Cards

Credit cards have become important financial tools since they provide consumers unprecedented spending power, flexibility, and convenience. Credit cards are complex tools, and in this chapter, we'll look into their numerous uses, possible disadvantages, and ways to make the most of them while protecting your money.

1. Convenience and Flexibility

Credit cards have transformed Indian customers' financial management by offering them before unprecedented convenience and flexibility. For Indian consumers, credit cards represent comfort and flexibility in the following ways:

A. **Seamless Transactions:** Credit cards streamline transactions, enabling users to make purchases online, in-store, or over the phone effortlessly. In India's rapidly digitizing economy, credit cards facilitate cashless transactions, reducing reliance on physical currency and enhancing payment convenience.

B. **Instant Access to Funds:** With a simple swipe or tap, credit cardholders gain instant access to funds, eliminating the need to carry large sums of cash or visit physical bank branches. This convenience is particularly advantageous in urban centers like Mumbai, Delhi, and Bengaluru, where cashless transactions are increasingly prevalent.

C. **Flexible Payment Options:** Credit cards offer users the flexibility to manage their payments according to their financial preferences. In India, cardholders can choose to pay the full outstanding amount by the due date to avoid interest charges or opt for minimum payments to spread the repayment over time. This flexibility empowers users to tailor their payment strategy based on their cash flow and financial commitments.

D. **Interest-Free Grace Periods:** Many credit cards in India provide interest-free grace periods, typically ranging from 20 to 50 days, during which cardholders can make purchases without incurring interest charges. This feature allows users to optimize their cash flow by deferring payments until the next billing cycle, thereby managing their expenses more efficiently.

E. **Secure Transactions:** Credit cards offer enhanced security elements meant to guard against fraud and illegal transactions, including two-factor authentication and EMV chip technology. This reassures users about the safety of their financial transactions, both online and offline, contributing to peace of mind and confidence in using credit cards.

2. Building and Enhancing Credit Score through Credit Cards

There are many benefits to applying for a credit card in India, including the capacity to build and enhance one's credit score. Here are some ways that prudent use of credit cards might improve credit scores in India:

A. **Timely Payments:** Making timely payments on credit card bills is essential for building a positive credit history. In India, consistent and punctual repayment of credit card dues demonstrates financial responsibility to credit bureaus, contributing to an improved credit score over time.

B. **Low Credit Utilization Ratios:** Maintaining low credit utilization ratios— the ratio of credit card balances to credit limits— is crucial for optimizing credit scores in India. By keeping credit card balances well below the available credit limits, cardholders can demonstrate responsible credit usage and lower risk to lenders, resulting in a positive impact on credit scores.

C. **Demonstrated Creditworthiness:** Responsible credit card usage allows individuals to showcase their creditworthiness and reliability to lenders and financial institutions in India. Consistent adherence to payment schedules and prudent management of credit limit reflects positively on credit reports, enhancing the likelihood of favourable terms on future loans, loans, and financial products.

D. **Access to Favourable Terms:** A robust credit score unlocks access to a host of financial benefits and opportunities in India, including lower interest rates, higher credit limits, and preferential terms on loans and loans. By building and enhancing their credit scores through responsible credit card usage, individuals can position themselves to avail of these favourable terms, thereby optimizing their financial well-being.

E. **Broadening Financial Opportunities:** A healthy credit score expands the scope of financial opportunities available to individuals in India. With an enhanced credit profile, cardholders gain access to a wider range of financial products and services, including premium credit cards, personal loans, and investment opportunities, empowering them to pursue their financial goals with confidence.

3. Privileges and Rewards

In India, credit cards offer a plethora of benefits that make banking simpler and more lucrative for cardholders. As an example of how credit card benefits and perks improve customers' lives.

A. **Cashback Incentives:** Many credit cards in India offer cashback rewards on various spending categories, including groceries, dining, fuel, and utility bills. These cashback incentives provide tangible savings for cardholders, effectively reducing their overall expenses and increasing purchasing power.

B. **Travel Perks:** Credit cards often come with travel-related perks such as air miles, airport lounge access, complimentary travel insurance, and hotel discounts. These benefits are particularly appealing to frequent travellers in India, enhancing their travel experiences and providing added convenience and security.

C. **Exclusive Discounts:** Cardholders can enjoy exclusive discounts and offers on shopping, dining, entertainment, and lifestyle experiences through their credit cards. These discounts may include special deals at partner merchants, online shopping portals, or local establishments, allowing users to save money while indulging in their favourite activities.

D. **Rewards Points and Miles:** Credit card users earn rewards points or miles on their spending, which can be accumulated and redeemed for a variety of rewards, including merchandise, gift vouchers, movie tickets, and flight bookings. This incentivizes card usage and provides cardholders with the flexibility to choose rewards that align with their preferences and interests.

E. **Premium Benefits:** Premium credit cards in India offer an array of exclusive benefits and privileges, catering to high-net-worth individuals and affluent customers. These may include personalized concierge services, priority customer support, golfing privileges, and access to VIP events, elevating the cardholder's lifestyle and providing a sense of prestige and exclusivity.

F. **Purchase Protection:** Many credit cards offer purchase protection benefits, such as extended warranty coverage, price protection, and fraud liability protection. These features provide cardholders with added peace of mind when making purchases, safeguarding them against unexpected expenses or fraudulent transactions.

4. Caveats and Considerations

There are many advantages to using a credit card, but there are also some hazards and obligations that Indian cardholders should think about. The following are important things to keep in mind:

A. **High-Interest Rates:** One of the most significant drawbacks of credit cards is the potential for high-interest rates, especially on outstanding balances. Failing to pay the full statement balance each month can result in accruing interest charges, leading to debt accumulation and financial strain over time. In India, where interest rates can be relatively high, users must prioritize timely repayment to avoid falling into a debt trap.

B. **Fees and Penalties:** Credit cards in India may entail various fees and penalties, including annual fees, late payment fees, and over-limit fees. These charges can accumulate quickly and significantly impact the cost of credit card usage, potentially outweighing any benefits or rewards earned. Users should familiarize themselves with the fee structure of their credit cards and strive to minimize unnecessary charges through responsible usage.

C. **Temptation to Overspend:** The convenience of credit cards can tempt individuals to overspend beyond their means, leading to debt accumulation and financial instability. In India's dynamic consumer landscape, where consumption patterns are evolving rapidly, it's crucial for users to exercise caution and discipline when using credit cards. Establishing a realistic budget, monitoring spending habits, and avoiding impulsive purchases can help mitigate the risk of overspending and debt accumulation.

D. **Credit Score Impact:** Responsible credit card usage can have a positive impact on one's credit score by demonstrating creditworthiness and reliability to lenders. However, missed payments, high credit utilization, or frequent applications for new credit cards can negatively affect credit scores in India. Users should be mindful of their credit behaviour and strive to maintain a healthy credit profile to access favorable terms on future loans and financial products.

E. **Security Concerns:** While credit cards offer enhanced security features such as EMV chip technology and two-factor authentication, they are not immune to fraud and unauthorized transactions. In India's rapidly digitizing economy, where online transactions are increasingly prevalent, users should remain vigilant against phishing scams, identity theft, and fraudulent activities. Regularly monitoring credit card statements, setting up transaction alerts, and adopting secure online practices can help mitigate security risks associated with credit card usage.

5. Strategic Planning and Management

Customers in India who want to get the most out of their credit cards should utilize them strategically. In order to keep credit card payments affordable and sustainable, it is necessary to plan, budget, and monitor spending closely. Here are some things customers can do to maximize their credit card spending:

A. **Create a Budget:** Start by creating a comprehensive budget that outlines your income, expenses, and financial goals. Identify areas where credit card usage can be optimized to maximize rewards and benefits while staying within budgetary constraints. Prioritize essential expenses and allocate a portion of your budget for discretionary spending, taking into account potential credit card payments.

B. **Track Expenses:** Regularly monitor your credit card transactions and track your expenses to stay informed about your spending patterns. Utilize mobile banking apps, online account portals, or expense tracking tools to categorize transactions, identify trends, and identify areas where spending can be optimized or reduced.

C. **Leverage Promotional Offers:** Take advantage of promotional offers, cashback deals, and reward programs offered by credit card issuers in India. Stay informed about ongoing promotions, discounts, and exclusive offers available to cardholders and strategically plan your purchases to maximize savings and rewards. Consider timing major purchases to coincide with promotional periods or festive seasons to optimize benefits.

D. **Optimize Reward Redemption:** Accumulate rewards points, miles, or cashback earned through credit card usage and strategically redeem them for maximum value. Evaluate the redemption options available, such as merchandise, gift vouchers, travel bookings, or statement credits, and choose the option that offers the best return on investment based on your preferences and requirements.

E. **Avoid Debt Locks:** Pay your credit card bills in full and on time each month to avoid accruing interest charges and minimize debt accumulation. Use credit cards as a payment tool rather than a source of financing, and resist the temptation to overspend beyond your means.

F. **Review and Adjust:** Regularly review your credit card usage, rewards, and financial goals to ensure alignment with your objectives and lifestyle. Assess the effectiveness of your credit card strategy, identify areas for improvement, and make adjustments as necessary to optimize your benefits and mitigate risks.

Chapter 6

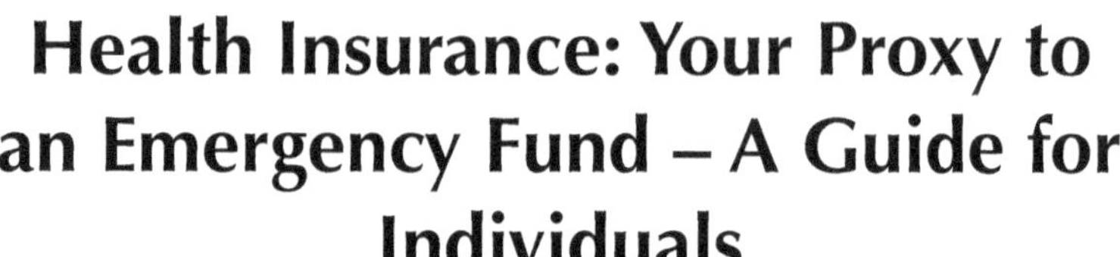

Health Insurance: Your Proxy to an Emergency Fund – A Guide for Individuals

When we focus on our financial security, health insurance is sometimes a secondary concern. Full health insurance is a need in India, where healthcare costs can quickly spiral out of control given the critical nature of medical treatment. To help you make educated decisions and protect your health and finances, I will walk you through the complexities of health insurance in India in this chapter, providing insights and practical recommendations.

1. Understanding Health Insurance in India

Health insurance in India operates within a unique regulatory and dynamic framework, influenced by the fact that the majority of the population uses both public and private healthcare facilities.

A. **Public Health Services:** The Indian government operates public health services aimed at providing basic healthcare facilities to the population, particularly in rural and underserved areas. These services include primary healthcare centers, community health centers, and district hospitals, offering essential medical care, vaccinations, and maternal and child health services.

B. **Dominance of Private Healthcare:** Despite the presence of public health services, the majority of Indians opt for private healthcare facilities due to perceived quality, accessibility, and availability of advanced medical treatments. Private hospitals and clinics, equipped with state-of-the-art infrastructure and specialized healthcare professionals, cater to a significant portion of the population's medical needs.

C. **Role of Health Insurance:** Health insurance plays a pivotal role in India's healthcare landscape, serving as a vital financial tool to mitigate the burden of healthcare expenses. Health insurance policies offer financial protection against unforeseen medical emergencies and ailments by covering hospitalization expenses, treatments, surgeries, diagnostic tests, medications, and other medical services.

D. **Coverage and Benefits:** Health insurance policies in India offer various coverage options and benefits tailored to the diverse needs of policyholders. Coverage typically includes inpatient hospitalization, daycare procedures, pre and post-hospitalization expenses, ambulance charges, and even alternative treatments like Ayurveda, Yoga, Naturopathy, Unani, Siddha, and Homeopathy (AYUSH) therapies in some cases.

E. **Premiums and Policy Features:** Health insurance premiums in India vary based on factors such as age, medical history, coverage limits, and add-on benefits. Policy features may include cashless hospitalization, reimbursement of medical expenses, critical illness coverage, maternity benefits, and coverage for pre-existing conditions, subject to waiting periods and terms specified in the policy.

F. **Government Initiatives:** The Indian government has launched several initiatives to promote health insurance coverage and increase access to healthcare services across the country. Programs such as Ayushman Bharat – Pradhan Mantri Jan Arogya Yojana (AB-PMJAY) aim to provide health insurance coverage to economically vulnerable households, offering financial protection against catastrophic healthcare expenses.

2. Types of Health Insurance Policies in India

In India, people and households have a choice of a selection of health insurance policies with varying degrees of coverage. You can choose from the following primary health insurance plans:

A. Individual Health Insurance

a. Provides coverage for medical expenses incurred by an individual policyholder. B.

b. Offers flexibility in choosing coverage limits, deductibles, and add-on benefits according to personal requirements.

B. Family Floater Plans

a. Covers the entire family under a single policy, with a predetermined sum insured shared among family members.

b. Offers convenience and cost-effectiveness compared to individual policies, as the sum insured can be utilized by any family member as per their medical needs.

C. Critical Illness Policies

a. Offers coverage for specific critical illnesses such as cancer, heart attack, stroke, organ transplant, and others.

b. Provides a lump sum payout upon diagnosis of a covered critical illness, helping policyholders manage treatment expenses and financial obligations. D.

D. Group Health Insurance

a. Provided by employers or associations for their employees or members.

b. Offers collective coverage for a group of individuals, typically at lower premiums compared to individual policies.

c. May include extra advantages including fitness initiatives, maternity coverage, and preventive health check-ups.

3. Key Features and Considerations when Selecting a Health Insurance Policy:

To make sure you're adequately covered and financially protected while purchasing a health insurance policy in India, you should think about these things

A. Sum Insured

a. Determine the maximum amount the insurer will pay for medical expenses.

b. Based on personal or family needs and expected medical expenses, select a sum insured that fairly covers possible healthcare costs.

B. Coverage

a. Review the policy coverage, including inpatient and outpatient treatments, pre-existing conditions, maternity benefits, and additional riders or add-ons.

b. Ensure the policy offers comprehensive coverage for a wide range of medical expenses, including hospitalization, surgeries, diagnostic tests, medications, and treatments.

C. Network Hospitals

a. Check the list of network hospitals covered by the insurer to ensure access to quality healthcare facilities in preferred locations.

b. Consider the geographical coverage and network strength of the insurer's empanelled hospitals for convenient and hassle-free cashless treatments.

D. Premiums

a. Evaluate premium costs and payment frequency to ensure affordability and sustainability over the long term.

b. Compare premium rates across different insurers and policy types while considering coverage benefits and features to make an informed decision.

E. Exclusions

    a. Understand the policy exclusions, including waiting periods, pre-existing conditions, specific treatments, and non-medical expenses.

    b. Be aware of any limitations or restrictions on coverage to avoid surprises during claim settlement and ensure transparency in policy terms and conditions.

4. Claim Process and Documentation:

In India, it is critical to understand the procedures for filing a claim and gathering the necessary papers in the event of a medical catastrophe. The Insurance Regulatory and Development Authority of India (IRDAI) has adopted a modification that will allow for 100% cashless claims beginning January 1, 2024. Understanding the revised processes is critical. The following is an outline of the claim procedure and documentation required.

Cashless Claim Process:

- Under the cashless claim process, policyholders can avail of medical treatment at network hospitals without making upfront payments, as the insurer directly settles the bills with the hospital.

- To initiate a cashless claim, inform the insurance company or Third-Party Administrator (TPA) about the hospitalization as soon as possible, preferably before admission.

- Present your health insurance card or policy details at the hospital's insurance desk to verify coverage and initiate the cashless claim process.

- The hospital will coordinate with the insurer or TPA to obtain pre-authorization for the treatment, specifying the estimated expenses and coverage details.

- Upon approval, the insurer will issue a pre-authorization letter to the hospital, allowing for cashless treatment up to the approved limit.

- Support from platforms like Policybazaar can be invaluable, especially if you purchase your policy through them. They provide complete support and guidance during the hospital admission process and allow for cashless claims, making the entire procedure more manageable.

5. Maximizing Benefits and Utilizing Preventive Care:

Health insurance in India not only provides financial protection during medical emergencies, but it also promotes preventive treatment and wellness programs.

Here's how policyholders can optimize benefits and use preventive treatment through their health insurance coverage:

A. Annual Health Check-ups

- Many health insurance policies include coverage for annual health check-ups or preventive screenings.

- Take advantage of these benefits to undergo comprehensive health assessments, including blood tests, diagnostic screenings, and consultations with healthcare professionals.

- Regular health check-ups can help detect underlying health conditions early, allowing for timely intervention and preventive measures.

B. Vaccination Coverage

- Some health insurance plans provide coverage for vaccinations, including routine immunizations and preventive vaccines.

- Ensure that you and your family members receive recommended vaccinations as per the immunization schedule to protect against vaccine-preventable diseases.

- Vaccination coverage under health insurance can help offset the cost of vaccines and encourage adherence to vaccination guidelines for optimal health outcomes.

C. Wellness Programs

- Many insurers offer wellness programs and initiatives aimed at promoting healthy lifestyles and preventive healthcare practices.

- Participate in wellness activities, health education sessions, and lifestyle management programs offered by insurers to improve overall health and well-being.

- Wellness programs may include fitness challenges, nutrition counseling, stress management techniques, and smoking cessation support, among other initiatives.

D. Health Risk Assessments

- Take advantage of health risk assessments provided by insurers to evaluate your current health status, identify potential risk factors, and develop personalized health improvement plans.

- Health risk assessments may involve questionnaire-based evaluations, biometric measurements, and lifestyle assessments to gauge overall health and disease risk.

E. Preventive Counseling and Education

- Seek preventive counseling and educational resources offered by insurers to gain insights into preventive healthcare measures and healthy living practices.

- Engage with healthcare professionals, nutritionists, and wellness experts through insurer-sponsored workshops, webinars, and educational materials to stay informed about preventive care strategies.

F. Healthy Lifestyle Incentives

- Some health insurance plans offer incentives or rewards for adopting healthy lifestyle behaviours and meeting wellness goals.

- Take advantage of incentives such as premium discounts, cashback rewards, or health credits for participating in wellness activities and achieving health targets.

6. Selecting the Best Health Insurance Plan: A Comprehensive Guide

When it comes to selecting a health insurance plan in India, it is important to carefully consider multiple factors to guarantee extensive coverage and financial stability. Here's a detailed guide that will help you choose the perfect health insurance plan that suits your specific requirements:

A. **No Cap on Room Rent:** Look for health insurance plans that do not impose a cap on room rent. Room rent limits can significantly impact your choice of hospital accommodation during treatment. Opting for a plan without room rent restrictions ensures flexibility and access to quality healthcare facilities without financial constraints.

B. **Minimal or No Waiting Period:** Choose a health insurance plan with minimal or no waiting period for coverage. Waiting periods can delay access to essential medical services, particularly for pre-existing conditions or specific treatments. Prioritize plans with shorter waiting periods or options to waive waiting periods for certain conditions.

C. **No Co-pay Requirement:** Avoid health insurance plans that impose co-pay requirements on policyholders. Co-payments require you to share a percentage of medical expenses out-of-pocket, increasing your financial burden during treatment. Opt for plans without co-pay clauses for comprehensive coverage and peace of mind.

D. **No Sublimit for Specific Treatments:** Ensure that your health insurance plan does not impose sublimits on specific treatments or services. Sublimits restrict the maximum amount payable for certain treatments, potentially leaving you underinsured in critical situations. Select plans with no sublimit clauses to ensure adequate coverage for all medical expenses.

E. **Comprehensive Coverage with No Waiting Periods:** Prioritize health insurance plans that offer comprehensive coverage without waiting periods. Comprehensive plans provide coverage for a wide range of medical services, including pre-existing conditions, maternity benefits, and critical illnesses, from the inception of the policy.

F. **Coverage for Consumable Items:** Look for health insurance plans that cover consumable items such as masks, gloves, and other medical supplies. In today's healthcare landscape, where hygiene and safety are paramount, coverage for consumable items ensures holistic protection against unforeseen medical expenses.

G. **Pre and Post-Hospitalization Expenses Coverage:** Select a health insurance plan that covers all charges associated with pre and post-hospitalization expenses. Pre and post-hospitalization coverage includes consultation fees, diagnostic tests, medications, and other related expenses incurred before and after hospitalization, providing comprehensive financial protection throughout your healthcare journey.

H. **Day Care Coverage for Technological Advancements:** Opt for a health insurance plan that offers day care coverage for medical treatments requiring less than 24 hours of hospitalization. With advancements in medical technology, many procedures no longer require prolonged hospital stays. Day care coverage ensures reimbursement for such treatments, offering flexibility and convenience for policyholders.

7. Additional Riders for Enhanced Coverage

Consider adding supplementary riders to your health insurance plan for enhanced coverage and additional benefits. Popular riders include:

- **Super Top-Up Rider:** Provides additional coverage beyond the base sum insured, offering financial protection against high medical expenses.

- **Restoration of Sum Assured:** Restores the sum insured amount once exhausted during the policy year, ensuring continuous coverage for subsequent medical expenses.

- **Unlimited Restoration:** Offers unlimited restoration of the sum insured amount, providing peace of mind in the event of multiple medical emergencies within the policy year.

8. Determining the Exact Sum Assured for Health Insurance Policies: Considering Medical Inflation and Benchmarking

It is essential that you select the right sum assured for your health insurance policy in order to ensure complete coverage and financial stability in the face of rising medical expenses. This section will guide you through the process of calculating the exact amount your health insurance policy guarantees, taking into account medical inflation and comparing it to the most expensive treatment in major cities.

Understanding Medical Inflation

The rate at which the cost of healthcare is rising over time has been referred to as medical inflation. Due to reasons like growing treatment costs, increased demand for healthcare services, and improvements in medical technology, medical inflation in India usually surpasses general inflation. To guarantee sufficient coverage for future medical requirements, it is crucial to take medical inflation into consideration when evaluating the sum assured for your health insurance policy.

Benchmarking Against Highest Treatment Costs

Try comparing your health insurance coverage to the highest treatment costs for different medical procedures in major cities to find the exact amount guaranteed. Due to variables like greater infrastructure expenditures, specialist fees, and state-of-the-art medical facilities, metro areas usually have higher healthcare bills. You may make sure your health insurance covers prospective medical bills in high-cost areas by benchmarking against the highest treatment prices in metro areas.

Steps to Determine Sum Assured

A. **Research Treatment Costs:** Research the average costs of medical procedures, hospitalization, and treatments in metro cities, considering factors such as hospital type, specialty, and geographic location.

B. **Factor in Medical Inflation:** Adjust the treatment costs for medical inflation to account for future increases in healthcare expenses. Use historical data on medical inflation rates to estimate future healthcare costs accurately.

C. **Evaluate Personal Health Risks:** Assess your personal health risks, medical history, and family medical history to identify potential health concerns and medical expenses that may arise in the future.

D. **Consider Lifestyle Factors:** Consider lifestyle factors such as age, occupation, dietary habits, and exercise routine that may impact your health and potential healthcare expenses.

E. **Consult with Insurance Advisor:** Seek guidance from an insurance advisor or financial planner to evaluate your insurance needs, assess coverage options, and determine the appropriate sum assured based on your individual circumstances.

To sum up, having good health insurance is a safety net, similar to having an emergency fund, because unexpected medical costs can quickly empty people's funds. Therefore, acquiring health insurance could be considered a prudent strategy to mitigate these financial risks.

Chapter 7

Understanding Term Insurance: A Vital Component of Financial Planning

When it comes to financial planning, protecting your loved ones' futures is crucial. Term insurance is essential for giving people and their families peace of mind and financial security. This chapter looks into the complexities of term insurance, examining its importance, advantages, and important factors to take into account while choosing the best coverage.

1. What is Term Insurance?

Term insurance is a type of pure life insurance that lasts for the policy term, which is an agreed-upon period of time. The insurer offers financial security and assistance during difficult times by paying the beneficiaries a predetermined sum assured in the event of the policyholder's death during the term.

Key Features of Term Insurance:

A popular choice for people looking for all-inclusive financial security at reasonable rates is term insurance.

Here are a few important features of term insurance plans:

1. Affordable Premiums

- Term insurance typically offers high coverage at relatively low premiums compared to other life insurance policies.

- Affordable premiums make term insurance accessible to a wide range of individuals, ensuring financial security for families and loved ones.

2. Pure Protection

- Term insurance provides pure protection or death benefit coverage without any investment or savings component.

- Unlike traditional life insurance policies, term insurance focuses solely on providing financial support to beneficiaries in the event of the policyholder's death.

3. Flexibility

- Term insurance policies offer flexibility in terms of policy duration, coverage amount, and premium payment options.

- Policyholders can choose the duration of coverage (term length), coverage amount (sum assured), and premium payment frequency (monthly, annually, etc.) based on their individual needs and preferences.

4. Customizable Riders

- Many term insurance plans offer customizable riders or add-on benefits that policyholders can include for enhanced coverage.

- Common riders include accidental death benefit rider, critical illness rider, waiver of premium rider, and income benefit rider, among others, allowing individuals to tailor their coverage to suit their specific requirements.

5. Tax Benefits

- Premiums paid towards term insurance policies are eligible for tax deductions under Section 80C of the Income Tax Act, up to specified limits.

- Additionally, the death benefit received by the nominee/beneficiary is tax-exempt under Section 10(10D) of the Income Tax Act, providing tax efficiency to policyholders.

6. Financial Security

- Term insurance gives policyholders financial stability and peace of mind by guaranteeing their loved ones' financial protection in the unfortunate event of the policyholder's passing.

- The death benefit received by the nominee/ beneficiary can help cover living expenses, loan payments, outstanding debts, children's education, and other financial obligations.

Benefits of Term Insurance

Term insurance has many advantages, giving policyholders and their loved one's peace of mind and financial security. The main benefits of term insurance are the following:

1. Financial Security

- Term insurance provides a financial safety net for your loved ones, ensuring that they are financially protected in the event of your untimely demise.

- The death benefit received by the nominee/ beneficiary can help cover living expenses, loan payments, outstanding debts, and other financial obligations, providing stability during a difficult time.

2. Debt Repayment

- The death benefit from term insurance can be utilized to repay outstanding debts such as home loans, personal loans, or credit card debts.

- By clearing debts with the insurance proceeds, you prevent the burden of repayment from falling on your family members, allowing them to maintain their financial independence and security.

3. Income Replacement

- Term insurance helps replace lost income due to the policyholder's death, ensuring that your family members can maintain their standard of living and meet daily expenses.

- The death benefit serves as a source of income replacement, enabling your family to cover essential costs, including household expenses, educational fees, healthcare bills, and other financial obligations.

4. Legacy Planning

- Term insurance allows you to leave a legacy for your loved ones, providing them with financial resources to pursue their dreams and aspirations even in your absence.

- By securing adequate coverage, you ensure that your family members have the means to achieve their long-term goals, whether it's funding higher education, starting a business, or securing their own financial future.

Selecting the Right Term Insurance Policy

To provide complete coverage and financial security for your loved ones, carefully evaluate a number of aspects while selecting the best term insurance policy. When choosing term insurance coverage, keep the following important things in mind:

1. Coverage Amount

- Determine the appropriate sum assured (coverage amount) based on your financial obligations, income level, and future needs of your family.

- Aim to secure a sum assured that is at least 25 times your annual earnings to provide adequate financial protection for your dependents in the event of your untimely demise.

- When determining your coverage requirements, take into account things including outstanding debt, loan payments, living expenses, inflation, and school costs.

2. Policy Term

- Select a policy term that aligns with your financial goals and the anticipated duration of your financial responsibilities.

- Longer policy terms provide extended coverage but may entail higher premiums, while shorter terms offer affordability but may leave your family vulnerable if the coverage expires before their financial needs are met.

- Evaluate your current age, retirement age, and the age of your dependents to determine the optimal policy term that ensures adequate protection throughout critical life stages.

3. Rider Options

- Explore additional riders or add-on benefits offered by the insurer to enhance your coverage and address specific needs.

- Common riders include critical illness cover, accidental death benefit, disability cover, income benefit rider, and premium waiver benefit, among others.

- Assess your lifestyle, health risks, and potential gaps in coverage to determine which riders are essential for your financial security and peace of mind.

4. Premium Affordability

- Evaluate the affordability of premiums based on your current income, budgetary constraints, and long-term financial commitments.

- While it's essential to secure adequate coverage, ensure that the premium payments are sustainable over the policy term to prevent lapses or termination of coverage.

- Examine the top quotations from several companies to identify competitive prices without sacrificing coverage or advantages.

5. Insurer's Reputation and Claim Settlement Record

- Research the insurer's reputation, financial stability, and claim settlement record to ensure reliability and trustworthiness.

- Choose an insurer with a strong track record of prompt and fair claim settlements, as this ensures that your beneficiaries receive the financial assistance they deserve without unnecessary delays or disputes.

The Drawbacks of Combining Investment Policies with Life Insurance

Even if the idea of combining investments and life insurance may appear enticing, it's important to be aware of the risks and disadvantages involved with purchasing such policies. This section explains why combining investments and life insurance might reduce their benefits and make it more difficult to achieve your long-term financial objectives.

Why Mixing Life Insurance with Investment Cab ne Detrimental

Although it may seem like a good idea to combine life insurance with investments, there are a number of risks and drawbacks to these kinds of products. This is the reason why combining investments with life insurance may be harmful.

1. Inadequate Coverage

- Policies that integrate life insurance with investment may provide insufficient coverage compared to standalone term insurance policies.

- The focus on generating investment returns may compromise the amount of coverage needed to adequately protect your family's financial future in the event of your untimely demise.

2. Higher Premiums

- Combining life insurance with investment often results in higher premiums compared to pure term insurance policies.

- A significant portion of the premium goes towards funding the investment component, reducing the overall coverage amount and value for money in terms of insurance protection.

3. Limited Investment Options

- Investment-linked insurance policies may offer limited investment options and lower returns compared to alternative investment avenues such as mutual funds or stocks.

- Policyholders may miss out on potential growth opportunities and higher returns available in the market by being restricted to the investment options provided by the insurance policy.

4. Complexity and Opacity

- Integrated insurance and investment policies often come with complex structures, hidden charges, and opaque terms and conditions.

- Understanding the intricacies of such policies can be challenging for policyholders, leading to confusion and potential mismanagement of funds.

- Hidden fees, surrender charges, and restrictions on withdrawals may erode the investment returns and reduce the overall value of the policy.

5. Lack of Flexibility

- Integrated policies may lack flexibility in terms of adjusting coverage levels or modifying investment strategies to align with changing financial goals and life circumstances.

- Policyholders may find themselves locked into rigid contracts with limited options for making adjustments or optimizing their insurance and investment portfolios.

6. Risk of Underperformance

- There's a risk that the investment component of the policy may underperform, failing to deliver the expected returns or even resulting in losses.

- Policyholders bear the investment risk, and poor market performance or economic downturns can negatively impact the value of their investment, affecting the overall financial security of their families.

The Importance of Separating Insurance and Investment

It's critical to understand that investments and insurance have distinct functions and need to be handled differently.

- **Insurance:** Provides financial protection and security for your loved ones in the event of your untimely demise.

- **Investment:** Aims to generate wealth and achieve long-term financial goals through strategic allocation of funds in diversified assets.

Chapter 8

The Web of Lies: Financial Scams

"My goal in this chapter is to expose several financial scams and how they work, so that you can be aware of potential dangers and take preventative measures." By bringing these fraudulent methods to light, we can better safeguard ourselves against financial fraud in the future.

1 – Courier Scam

Typically, in the early hours of the morning, an apparently innocent phone call sets off the staged FedEx scam. A voice that appears to be speaking for FedEx approaches gullible people, sparking a discussion that lays the groundwork for a terrifying experience.

The caller starts off by asking, "Have you recently used FedEx to send a courier to Taiwan?" in an apparent innocent manner. This seemingly innocent question is the starting point for a complex web of lies. The caller discloses a troubling development in the story after the victim denies any involvement in such overseas transactions.

The caller delivers a shocking revelation in an urgent tone: a malicious scheme has fraudulently used the victim's Aadhar card number. Claims suggest the smuggling of illegal goods, including substances like MDMA and LSD, to distant locations using the victim's name. The victim, shocked and confused, calls for help, and the caller suggests taking quick action.

The caller offers a direct line of communication to the cybercrime team as a way to address the issue. Smoothly transitioning the call to a purported cybercrime police officer, the caller assures the victim that this step is essential to resolving the issue.

This is where the appearance of legitimacy starts to fade. They force the victim to divulge private financial information under the pretence of conducting an inquiry. Empty promises of revealing the truth and proving the victim's innocence conceal the underlying purpose of the deceit. At this crucial point, the victim starts to feel instinctively uneasy because they can sense something evil lurking beneath the surface of power.

The victim has a flash of insight and understands that they have been duped by a well-planned con game. A cloud of doubt descends over the victim's mind as the call comes to an end, casting a pall over their feelings of betrayal.

Following the encounter, the victim seeks solace via the internet and searches for answers. Here, they discover stories of people who become entangled in the same web of lies and have their lives turned upside down by the vicious schemes of online fraudsters. It is both a sad reminder of the ongoing menace that lurks in the digital shadows and an appeal to awareness and vigilance against fraud.

As the sun sets on another day, the victim emerges from the trauma, their resolve reinforced by the difficult lessons learned. They are a light of knowledge in a dangerous world, and they serve as a reminder of the human spirit's resiliency even if they are still traumatized from the experience.

2 – Bank Phishing Scam

An internet search is the first step in the malicious bank phishing scam's destructive path. Upon navigating to the website of their trusted financial institution, gullible people are greeted with an apparently authentic search result. They don't realize, though, that this mild inquiry sets them up for a dangerous encounter with cybercriminals.

When consumers click on the fraudulent search result, they are taken to a carefully constructed spoof website that replicates the look and feel of the official bank website. The fake website looks exactly like the real one, giving customers a false sense of security with its well-designed UI and convincing branding.

When customers land on the fake website, they are asked to provide their login information—password and customer ID—while pretending to be logging into their bank account. Unaware of the danger waiting beyond the surface, gullible people easily fall into the trap that has been laid in front of them.

The user is unaware that the crooks behind the scam quickly obtained their private details. Once the fraudsters obtain the victim's customer ID and password, they can easily access the victim's bank account and cause significant damage to their financial resources.

Once inside the victim's account, the fraudsters get right to work, carrying out their malicious plan. They carefully extract money from the hacked account, transferring hard-earned savings into their personal accounts and showing no concern for the consequences of their conduct.

The effects of the bank phishing scam are devastating for the victim. What started off as an ordinary internet transaction has turned into a nightmare involving a loss of money and psychological trauma. They are left to deal with the terrible reality of betrayal at the hands of invisible enemies after being deprived of their financial security.

However, there is still a glimmer of optimism despite all the chaos and sorrow. Users can protect themselves from falling victim to these sneaky scams by being proactive in verifying the legitimacy of bank websites. Easy precautions against the schemes of cybercriminals can include checking the website for evidence of modification and confirming that the URL is encrypted with HTTPS.

Vigilance and awareness continue to be our greatest allies in the fight against cybercrime as the digital world changes. With a careful and well-informed approach to our online interactions, we can safeguard ourselves and our loved ones from the serious consequences of bank phishing scams.

3 – Customer Care Scam

A fraudulent method used by cybercriminals, the customer care scam preys on gullible people who contact reputable businesses for assistance. A straightforward social media request for assistance soon turns into a nightmare of monetary loss and psychological trauma.

Innocent people contact company assistance via social media platforms, disclosing personal information such as addresses and phone numbers in the hopes of having their complaints addressed. This is how the scam works. They have no idea that the seemingly innocent posts they make serve as a lure for criminals who lurk in the shadows of the internet.

Scammers have created advanced software that searches social networking sites for posts that include private information. As soon as they see a victim's cry for assistance, they respond quickly, disguising themselves as official company employees in order to carry out their fraudulent scheme.

Equipped with the victim's personal information and the legitimacy of the business's social media account, the con artist contacts the gullible person. Because it comes from the same platform where they requested assistance from the company, the victim believes the call or message to be authentic.

The con artist deceives the victim into believing they are safe with sweet talk and quick fixes. They entice the victim with the promise of a fast reimbursement or resolution to their complaint, assuring them that their problem will be promptly addressed.

In a complex turn of events, the con artist convinces the victim to download a third-party viewer app that appears to be harmless on their smartphone. Under the pretence of offering remote assistance, the victim unknowingly grants the scammer access to their device, potentially storing sensitive banking information.

After deceiving the victim, the con artist proceeds quickly to carry out their nefarious plan. With the victim's smartphone securely in their grasp, they take money out of their bank account and cause havoc in their wake. In the aftermath, the customer care fraud leaves a trail of financial loss and psychological anguish. The victims are left to deal with the terrible truth of their betrayal, their confidence destroyed by invisible enemies disguising themselves as legitimate.

There is, however, an appearance of optimism amid the chaos and misery. People can protect themselves from these sneaky frauds by being cautious and refraining from disclosing personal information on social media sites. Easy precautions, such as confirming the authenticity of customer support channels and avoiding downloading unknown software, can be effective barriers against the schemes of cybercriminals. Vigilance and awareness continue to be our greatest allies in the fight against cybercrime as the digital world changes.

4 – Olx/Marketplace scams

Popular used-item marketplace OLX has become a safe haven for fraudsters looking to take advantage of gullible people. A straightforward transaction between a buyer and a seller has the potential to turn swiftly into a nightmare of fraud and monetary loss.

OLX scams often begin with enticing offers that appear excessively attractive. Attracted by tempting pricing, purchasers eventually become prey to complex plots intended to defraud them of their hard-earned cash.

One typical situation is salespeople going undercover as members of the armed forces or as professionals, such as doctors, and taking advantage of the respect and confidence these occupations command to trick unsuspecting buyers. These con artists create a sense of urgency that forces purchasers to move quickly without doing due diligence by making up stories of urgency, such as impending relocation or financial difficulty.

Sometimes, sellers use an urgent situation—like leaving the country soon—to justify their absurdly low price. Scammers may even offer fictitious documentation and pictures of the supposed car in order to give their claims more credibility. But these claims fall apart when examined more closely, exposing a complex network of lies and manipulation.

Scammers employ a particularly cunning tactic when they claim that the airport authorities have seized the car they are selling due to unpaid parking fees. Scammers instruct buyers to reclaim the vehicle by paying fictitious parking tickets and fees.

Unsuspecting buyers may give in to the scammer's demands in a last-ditch attempt to salvage what they perceive to be a good deal, only to end up broke and without any money. A profitable arrangement that seems promising might suddenly turn into a nightmare of lost money and psychological suffering.

Buyers should exercise caution and scepticism when encountering deals that appear excessively attractive to avoid falling prey to OLX scams and marketplace fraud.

One way to reduce the likelihood of falling victim to fraudulent schemes is to meet dealers in public areas and perform extensive background checks.

5 – Telegram Job Scams

Job seekers in the digital age frequently use online platforms to find opportunities, and Telegram has become a popular spot to network and find job posts. But within the genuine job postings is a web of lies created by con artists that feed off the dreams and wishes of gullible people.

Typically, the strategy behind Telegram employment scams starts with alluring job offers that guarantee high compensation and interesting career opportunities. These job postings seem authentic at first glance, with thorough job descriptions and convincing language luring individuals to submit. They are frequently posted in Telegram groups or channels dedicated to job seekers.

Job seekers are unaware that these alluring offers are nothing more than sophisticated scams designed to trick and exploit them. Scammers use Telegram's anonymity to further their dishonest goals with impunity, posing as hiring managers or recruiters.

Job seekers receive instructions to initiate private messaging with the scammer upon expressing interest in a specific opportunity. Here, the scammer assumes the identity of a reputable employer and starts having discussions with the victim in an attempt to gain rapport and confidence.

Under the pretext of finalizing the employment process, con artists occasionally ask job seekers for personal information or supporting papers. Gullible people easily fall into the trap, unaware of the danger lurking beneath the surface.

The con artist may introduce more conditions or processes throughout the chat, such as paying registration fees or finishing online tests. These requests act as warning signs that reveal the true nature of the fraud because they are made under the pretext of normal recruiting procedures.

Some job seekers may give in to pressure and agree with the scammer's requests in a desperate attempt to land the promised employment opportunity, only to find themselves the victims of identity theft and financial loss.

To avoid falling victim to Telegram job scams, job seekers should exercise caution and scepticism towards employment offers that appear excessively attractive. One can lessen the likelihood of falling for fraudulent schemes by doing extensive research on the organization and recruiter, confirming the authenticity of job advertising, abstaining from disclosing personal information, and not making payments up front.

6 – Loan App Scams

In the realm of technology, where convenience often clashes with dependence, the proliferation of loan applications has spawned a new form of fraud targeting unsuspecting individuals in dire financial need. Under the pretext of accessibility and ease, these fraudulent tactics prey on the desperation of borrowers, wreaking havoc and suffering in the aftermath.

These loan applications seem innocent at first glance, providing quick and simple cash access with little paperwork and no credit checks. Beneath the surface, however, is a dark realm of exploitation and deceit, where gullible borrowers become entangled in a web of lies from which they seem powerless to free themselves.

The broad access and permissions that these apps request when downloaded is one of the distinguishing characteristics of loan app scams. These apps seek access to private chat apps, contacts, images, and other sensitive data in their search for personal information, setting the stage for future extortion and blackmail. This sneaky method, which seems to be a requirement for loan acceptance, lays the groundwork for the exploitation of weaker people.

Exorbitant interest rates and hidden fees spin out of control, trapping the victims of these scams in a never-ending cycle of debt and guilt. Borrowers with poor credit sometimes face interest rates as high as 100%, which can make even a little loan into an overwhelming debt that could eventually engulf them.

When borrowers try to return their loans, the lending app's administrators confront them with more threats and blackmail, which exposes the full scope of fraud. Scammers use chat apps and personal contacts to spread modified photographs and videos to harass and blackmail victims into paying more money.

Beyond just suffering a financial loss, becoming a victim of loan app scams can have a lasting negative impact on one's reputation and cause mental misery. What started out as a search for financial support turns into a nightmare of fraud and abuse, leaving victims in shock at the betrayal of their confidence. Because of these sneaky hazards, people must exercise caution and doubt when interacting with lending apps and financial services. Borrowers should look into traditional lending channels instead of giving in to the attraction of instant cash, as these channels place a higher value on duty and transparency.

7– Mobile Sim-card swap scam

With our lives becoming more and more connected with technology in today's connected world, the Sim Card Swap Scam serves as a terrifying reminder of the risks that are located beneath the surface of our digital existence. This sneaky plan seriously jeopardizes our financial and personal security by taking advantage of the core architecture of our mobile communication networks.

The Sim Card Swap Scam's primary method is the covert activation of a new SIM card that is connected to the victim's account in order to manipulate the victim's mobile phone number. Insider cooperation or social engineering techniques frequently enable this evil deed, essentially giving the attacker complete control over the victim's digital and mobile accounts.

The power to capture private data, take over internet accounts, and carry out identity theft and financial crime without detection is a far-reaching and disastrous consequence of such access. The fraudster can reset passwords, get around two-factor authentication, and access social media, bank, and email accounts without authorization if they have the victim's mobile number.

The Sim Card Swap Scam usually involves multiple steps. The first involves obtaining the victim's personal information through phishing emails, social media reconnaissance, or data breaches, among other methods. Equipped with this data, the con artist contacts the victim's mobile provider and asks for a replacement, using a believable excuse like a misplaced or broken SIM card.

Scammers also frequently pose as customer service representatives from the victim's mobile network provider, though. The scammer coerces the victim into disclosing private information or unintentionally approving the activation of a new Sim card under the pretext of helping them with a supposed Sim card upgrade to 4G or 5G. The con artist gains the upper hand in carrying out their fraudulent plan by taking advantage of the victim's confidence and tricking them into providing their agreement under pretext.

The fraudster takes control of the victim's incoming calls and texts after activating the new SIM card and connecting it to their phone number. This allows them to successfully intercept private data and authentication codes supplied over SMS. This access enables the scammer to engage in illicit activities, modify passwords, and gain entry to the victim's digital accounts, all while remaining undetected.

The Sim Card Swap Scams have severe repercussions that can include loss of money, harm to one's reputation, and psychological suffering. Victims may find themselves unable to access their own accounts, rendering them powerless to prevent fraudulent activities in their name and unauthorized access.

People need to be cautious and watchful when protecting their digital accounts and personal information to avoid becoming victims of the Sim Card Swap Scam. Putting strong security measures in place, such as protecting mobile accounts with a PIN or password, monitoring account activity for unusual activity, and promptly reporting any unwanted access to mobile service providers and appropriate authorities, is necessary.

When navigating its vast extent, one cannot ignore the plethora of frauds that lie in the shadows of the internet world. During this discussion, we explored the various aspects of numerous fraudulent schemes, all of which aim to take advantage of the gullible and profit at the expense of other people's security and trust.

These depressing stories, in fact, serve as frightening reminders of how crucial it is to protect oneself from the dangers of internet fraud. There are several ways in which the proverb "money saved is money earned" applies to wealth management and finance. Every rupee that is kept out of the hands of con artists is an achievement in the fight for stability and financial security.

Reading through the book's chapters, you're not just learning about financial concepts and procedures; you're also equipping yourself with the knowledge and skills required to successfully negotiate the dangerous landscape of the digital age. You are laying the groundwork for a prosperous and peaceful future by fortifying your defences against scams and fraud. Recall that every lesson you take away from this experience serves as a defence against the threats that exist online. Turning each page gives you more power to safeguard your financial stability and make wise decisions. Let's begin on the path to financial security and literacy together, creating a better, more secure future.

Chapter 9

Penny Wise, Pound Foolish: Understanding the Pitfalls of Short-Term Savings

The proverb "penny wise, pound foolish" is a cautionary tale in the world of personal finance, warning us against the risks involved in putting short-term savings ahead of long-term financial security. This chapter explores the subtle aspects of this idea, showing how people in India frequently give in to the temptation of instant gratification at the expense of their long-term financial security.

1. The Temptation of Frugality

Frugality is highly regarded in India, a nation known for its diversity and vibrancy, as people take great pride in their ability to stretch a rupee to its limit. Indians are experts at making short-term financial savings; from haggling over vegetable pricing at the neighbourhood market to searching online marketplaces for the best offers.

Example: Buying Low-Quality Goods

Think about the situation where you buy cheap products just because they are affordable. Even though the initial cost savings would seem alluring, people might find that they need to replace these things more frequently because of their poor quality, which would result in higher long-term costs.

Detailing the Consequences

Higher Long-Term Costs: Although opting for cheaper alternatives might save money initially, the need for frequent replacements can lead to higher long-term expenses. Buying cheap electronics or household goods, for example, may lead to frequent malfunctions or breakdowns, requiring expensive repairs or replacements.

Decreased Satisfaction and Convenience: Low-quality goods may fail to perform as expected, causing frustration and inconvenience. A mediocre piece of clothing, a broken device, or shoddy furnishings can all have a negative impact on one's overall quality of life due to their unsatisfactory nature and associated difficulties.

Striking a Balance

Achieving sustainability requires finding a balance between immediate cost reductions and long-term benefits. When making purchases, people should take longevity, dependability, and general quality into account rather than just the initial cost. Individuals can steer clear of the traps associated with frugal living and ultimately obtain better value for their hard-earned money by making investments in higher-quality products that provide durability and happiness.

2. Neglecting Financial Planning

Despite their tendency for savings, a large number of Indians neglect to give long-term financial planning the attention it deserves in favour of short-term savings and expenses. This narrow-minded strategy frequently leads to lost chances for future wealth creation and financial stability.

Example: Avoiding Insurance Premiums

Reluctance to invest in insurance coverage, such as health or life insurance, is one classic example of this problem. Even though the premiums might appear expensive now, not having insurance in the event of an emergency might have disastrous long-term financial effects.

3. Ignoring Investment Opportunities

There are many investment options in India, an economy that is changing quickly and has the potential to yield large profits over time. Those who put short-term savings ahead of long-term investments, however, can pass up these chances, which would hinder their capacity to accumulate wealth and meet their financial objectives.

Example: Hoarding Cash Instead of Investing

Some people may choose to hoard cash or place their savings in low-interest accounts rather than investing their money in stocks, mutual funds, or real estate. In the short run, this might give you a sense of security, but it doesn't take advantage of compound interest and returns that beat inflation on long-term investments.

4. Sacrificing Education and Skill Development

Ongoing education and skill development are crucial for staying relevant and competitive in a labour market that is changing quickly. On the other hand, people who put short-term savings ahead of investing in their education and skill development may find that they are ill-prepared to keep up with the rapidly evolving technology landscape and shifting industrial trends.

Example: Opting for Low-Cost Training Programs

Some people might choose to use free or inexpensive but questionable alternatives in place of authorized training programs or respectable educational institutions, which may demand a larger initial outlay of funds. These programs might save money right now, but they might not have the depth and reputation that will improve a person's professional opportunities over time.

In summary, while short-term savings are unquestionably necessary, it's also important to take a balanced approach that puts long-term financial growth and stability first. People can guarantee their financial future and attain long-lasting wealth by realizing the dangers of "penny wise, pound foolish" behaviour and making investments in insurance, education, and wise investments.

Chapter 10

Navigating the Terrain of an Emerging Economy: Insights from India

As demonstrated by nations like India, the emerging economy environment offers a dynamic mosaic of opportunities and difficulties, with the complexity of development entangled with the promise of prosperity. This chapter explores the complexities of negotiating the environment of a growing economy, providing thoughts and insights from the Indian experience.

1. The Promise of Growth

The core of a rising economy is its potential for expansion, which attracts both investors and business owners. A growing middle class, increasing urbanization, and technological improvements fuel India's growing consumer market. This provides an ideal environment for businesses to flourish and grow.

Example: E-commerce Boom

The emergence of e-commerce behemoths such as Flipkart and Amazon India highlight the revolutionizing influence of technology on the Indian economy. Online shopping has increased dramatically as a result of millions of people getting access to smartphones and the internet, upending preconceived notions about traditional retail and promoting a thriving digital economy.

2. The Challenge of Inequality

However, the danger of inequality, a widespread problem that threatens to sever the social fabric of emerging nations, looms alongside the promise of progress. Income, opportunity, and resource disparities cause rifts in society that impede inclusive progress and exacerbate social unrest.

Example: Digital Divide

India is experiencing a digital revolution that has the ability to close disparities and empower access to services and information. However, the digital gap still exists, with marginalized and rural people experiencing obstacles to digital literacy and internet access. We must address this inequality to fully realize India's digital transformation potential.

3. The Imperative of Sustainable Development

Sustainable development is becoming more and more important as emerging economies steer towards expansion. To ensure long-term prosperity and resilience in the face of global problems, it is crucial to strike a balance between economic advancement, environmental conservation, and social equality.

Example: Renewable Energy Initiatives

India's bold efforts in the field of renewable energy, such as the National Solar Mission and the promotion of wind power, are prime examples of the nation's dedication to sustainable development. India seeks to slow down climate change while also promoting economic growth by reducing its dependence on fossil fuels and investing in clean energy infrastructure.

4. The Role of Innovation and Entrepreneurship

When negotiating the intricacies of a developing market, innovation and entrepreneurship show themselves to be powerful agents of advancement. Emerging economies have the potential to provide new avenues for growth, propel technological progress, and promote economic diversification by promoting a culture that values innovation, risk-taking, and cooperation.

Example: Startup Ecosystem

India's flourishing startup scene, which is concentrated in places like Hyderabad and Bengaluru, highlights the revolutionary power of entrepreneurship and innovation. Indian entrepreneurs are bringing substantial change and influencing the direction of the economy, from innovative technology firms to social enterprises addressing important societal issues.

In conclusion, it takes advanced knowledge of the opportunities and challenges of a growing country like India to successfully navigate its terrain. Emerging economies may pave the way for equitable and sustainable prosperity by utilizing the potential of growth, tackling inequality, promoting sustainable development, and encouraging innovation and entrepreneurship.

Chapter 11

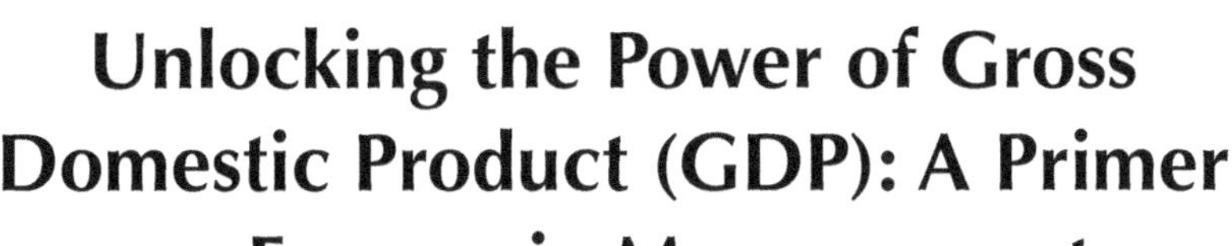

Unlocking the Power of Gross Domestic Product (GDP): A Primer on Economic Measurement

Gross Domestic Product (GDP) is a fundamental concept in economic assessment that is used to evaluate the strength and health of a country's economy. This chapter takes us on a quest to discover the GDP's hidden meanings and applications for comprehending economic activity and prosperity.

1. Understanding GDP

The Gross Domestic Product (GDP) is a critical indicator in economic analysis because it provides a comprehensive picture of an economy's size, health, and performance. In its most basic form, GDP represents the total monetary value of all products and services produced within a nation's boundaries over a specific time period, typically calculated on a quarterly basis.

Example: Components of GDP

Breaking down the concept of GDP unveils its intricate composition, comprising several key components that collectively contribute to economic activity:

- **Consumer Spending**: Consumer expenditure represents the total spending by households on goods and services, ranging from groceries and clothing to healthcare and entertainment. Consumer spending serves as a primary driver of economic growth, reflecting the demand for goods and services within the economy.

- **Business Investment**: Business investment encompasses capital expenditures by businesses on machinery, equipment, infrastructure, and other productive assets. Investments in technology, innovation, and expansion initiatives fuel productivity gains and drive long-term economic growth.

- **Government Expenditures**: Government expenditures encompass spending by the public sector on goods and services, including Defense, Infrastructure, Education, Healthcare, and social welfare programs. Government spending plays a vital role in stimulating economic activity, particularly during periods of recession or stagnation.

- **Net Exports**: Net exports represent the difference between a country's exports and imports of goods and services. A positive net export balance indicates that the value of exports exceeds imports, contributing positively to GDP. Conversely, a negative net export balance implies a trade deficit, subtracting from GDP.

Analysts and decision-makers can learn a great deal about the fundamental forces behind economic development, investment and consumption trends, government actions, and the state of the economy as a whole by breaking down these GDP components. Comprehending the complex interactions among these elements is crucial for devising efficient economic strategies, promoting sustainable growth, and augmenting the welfare of the populace.

2. Significance of GDP

GDP is essential to calculating economic policy, evaluating living standards, and comparing the relative economic performance of different countries. GDP, a comprehensive indicator of economic activity, provides important information about an economy's state and future direction.

Example: GDP Growth Rate

The growth rate is one of the most important measures obtained from GDP and is a crucial indicator of the condition and direction of the economy. Usually calculated annually or quarterly, the GDP growth rate represents the percentage change in economic output over a specified time period.

- **Positive Growth**: A positive GDP growth rate signals expansion and prosperity within an economy. It indicates that the total value of goods and services produced has increased compared to the previous period. Positive GDP growth fosters optimism, as it signifies rising incomes, employment opportunities, and overall economic well-being. Policymakers often strive to achieve sustainable positive growth rates to support development goals and enhance living standards.

- **Negative Growth**: Conversely, a negative GDP growth rate, also known as economic contraction, denotes a decline in economic output. Negative growth rates may result from factors such as recessionary pressures, supply disruptions, or external shocks. Economic contractions can lead to job losses, income reduction, and diminished consumer confidence, posing challenges for individuals, businesses, and governments. Policymakers typically implement counter-cyclical measures to stimulate economic activity and mitigate the adverse effects of negative growth.

By monitoring GDP growth rates, policymakers can evaluate an economy's resilience, identify emerging trends, and adjust their policy measures accordingly. Furthermore, examining GDP growth rates among other nations provides valuable information about their respective economic performance, competitiveness, and development paths. In general, the GDP growth rate is a vital indicator of the state of the economy, influencing strategic choices and setting policy objectives with the goal of achieving sustainable growth and prosperity.

3. Methodologies of GDP Calculation

Compiling a nation's GDP requires sophisticated techniques designed to account for the wide range of economic activities that take place there. The production approach, income approach, and expenditure approach are some of these techniques that provide different insights into economic output.

Example: Production Approach

The production approach, which explores the complex web of value creation across several economic sectors, is a fundamental technique for estimating GDP. The production approach's primary goal is to measure the value contributed at every stage of the manufacturing process, from raw materials to final goods and services.

- **Value Addition**: Under the production approach, economists track the incremental value generated by each economic unit along the production chain. This value addition accounts for the difference between the value of inputs (e.g., raw materials, labour) and the value of outputs (e.g., final goods, services). By aggregating these value-added contributions across all sectors of the economy, economists derive an estimate of total economic output.

- **Sectoral Analysis**: The production approach allows for a granular examination of economic activity, facilitating sectoral analysis and insights into industry-specific trends. Economists dissect production data to discern patterns of growth, identify emerging sectors, and assess the relative contributions of different industries to overall GDP.

- **Challenges and Considerations**: While the production approach provides valuable insights into the structure and dynamics of an economy, it is not without its challenges. Accurately measuring value added at each stage of production requires comprehensive data collection, which may pose logistical and methodological hurdles. Additionally, the production approach may overlook informal or unrecorded economic activities, leading to potential underestimation of GDP.

Economists may establish a comprehensive understanding of economic output by combining complementary approaches with the production approach. This allows policymakers to develop evidence-based plans for development, growth, and overall economic well-being.

4. Implications of GDP

GDP estimates influence public views of wealth and well-being in addition to informing decisions on economic policy. However, because of these limits, GDP measurements may not adequately account for factors such as income distribution, environmental sustainability, and economic welfare.

Example: GDP and Quality of Life

Despite its use in evaluating economic output and activity, the usefulness of GDP as an indicator of general societal well-being remains disputed. When assessing factors related to a society's quality of life, economic distribution, and accessibility to basic amenities, the limitations of GDP become evident.

- **Distribution of Wealth**: GDP fails to capture the distribution of wealth within a society, offering little insight into income inequality and disparities in wealth accumulation. Thus, a nation may boast impressive GDP figures while simultaneously grappling with widening income gaps and social stratification.

- **Access to Services**: Despite robust GDP growth, certain segments of the population may lack access to essential services such as healthcare, education, and sanitation. In such cases, GDP metrics may overstate societal well-being by overlooking disparities in access and quality of services across different socioeconomic groups.

- **Environmental Sustainability**: GDP metrics often disregard the environmental costs associated with economic activity, leading to a skewed perception of progress. While GDP growth may signal economic prosperity, it may come at the expense of natural resources depletion, pollution, and ecological degradation, undermining long-term sustainability.

To sum up, GDP is a fundamental tool for measuring economic activity and provides important information about an economy's size, development, and function. When we understand GDP's limitations, importance, and intricate calculations, we can better appreciate its role in influencing public and economic policy.

Chapter 12

Unraveling Inflation: Understanding its Impacts and Implications

Macroeconomic research relies heavily on inflation, which affects firms, consumers, and policymakers in equal measure. This chapter takes us on a journey into the intricacies of inflation, examining its origins, effects, and ramifications in light of India's economic situation.

1. Understanding Inflation

Fundamentally, inflation is the gradual but steady rise in the average cost of goods and services over time. Money loses purchasing power, raising costs for both consumers and businesses. Comprehending the factors that contribute to inflation is essential for developing efficient fiscal and monetary strategies that uphold price stability.

Example: Demand-Pull and Cost-Push Inflation

Demand-pull and cost-push forces frequently work together to create inflationary pressures in India. Demand-pull inflation drives prices higher when total demand exceeds total supply. On the other hand, cost-push inflation arises from the transfer of rising production expenses, such as labour costs or raw material prices, to customers.

2. Impacts of Inflation

Across a number of economic sectors, inflation has a knock-on effect on people, businesses, and the macroeconomic environment as a whole. While low to moderate inflation can encourage investment and economic growth, high or fluctuating inflation presents serious problems, such as diminished purchasing power, business instability, and imbalances in the distribution of resources.

Example: Wage-Price Spiral

Inflation can trigger a wage-price spiral, where workers seek greater pay to maintain their quality of life due to rising prices. This, in turn, drives up manufacturing costs for companies, resulting in more price hikes and feeding the inflationary cycle. To break this cycle, it will need aggressive steps to address the underlying inflationary pressures.

3. Policy Responses to Inflation

To control inflation and preserve price stability, governments and central banks utilize a variety of monetary and fiscal policy instruments. A few of these could be changing interest rates, enacting specific budgetary cuts, and using macroprudential rules to reduce inflationary pressures and stabilize the economy.

Example: Monetary Policy and Inflation Targeting

In order to manage inflation and stabilize inflation expectations, the Reserve Bank of India (RBI) in India uses inflation targeting as a crucial policy tool. In order to meet its inflation targets, the RBI seeks to regulate liquidity in the financial system and affect borrowing and spending patterns through tools including the repo rate and open market operations.

4. Inflation in the Indian Context

Numerous factors, such as external shocks, structural limitations, and demographic patterns, influence India's experience with inflation. To effectively handle inflation's repercussions and ramifications, governments, businesses, and individuals alike must have a thorough understanding of the complexities of inflation dynamics in the Indian environment.

Example: Food Inflation and Supply Chain Disruptions

Due to the nation's reliance on imports of food and agriculture, food inflation frequently becomes a major contributor to total inflationary pressures in India. Supply chain disruptions, such as bad weather or logistical difficulties, can exacerbate food price volatility and lead to more general inflationary trends.

5. The Erosion of Purchasing Power: A Case Study

Let's look at a hypothetical example of a 1 crore INR declining in value over time as a result of inflation. The buying power of one crore would decline dramatically over the following time periods, assuming an average inflation rate of 7%:

- **10 years from now:** The value of 1 Crore would be equivalent to approximately 50 Lakhs.

- **15 years from now:** The value would further decline to around 36 Lakhs.

- **20 years from now:** It would diminish to approximately 25 Lakhs.

The example provided illustrates how sneaky inflation can be and how critical it is to effectively manage its effects on investments and personal money.

6. The Crucial Intersection of Wealth and Inflation

A recurring concern for people looking to achieve financial independence and stability in their later years is retirement planning. However, the response to this question goes beyond simple statistics, as it depends on the dynamic interaction of inflationary pressures, investment plans, and wealth generation.

A. The Illusion of Absolute Wealth

Many people make the mistake of associating financial stability with their absolute wealth, thinking that having a sizable amount of money in their bank accounts guarantees a relaxing retirement. This idea, however, ignores the subtle effects of inflation, which gradually reduces the purchasing value of money. If inflation exceeds investment returns, even a fortune worth 100 crores today may lose value, leaving people vulnerable to a steady erosion of their money.

B. Confronting the Reality of Inflation

The silent enemy of wealth preservation, inflation, presents a serious obstacle to both investors and retirees. Prices that rise faster than investment returns jeopardize long-term financial security. This is because money loses its real value over time. Unless people take aggressive steps to combat inflationary pressures, they face the terrifying possibility of losing all their money in a scenario where investments yield a meager 10% return and real inflation soars to 20%.

C. The Imperative of Investment Mastery

A grasp of investment ideas and methods is a prerequisite for navigating the perilous waters of retirement planning. In an inflationary environment, investors need to look for ways to grow their wealth faster than the rate of inflation. Simply putting money away in a savings account or fixed deposit will not cut it. Investing in a variety of asset types, inflation-linked instruments, and stocks allows investors to take advantage of compound interest to produce returns that outpace inflationary benchmarks.

D. Charting a Course Towards Financial Freedom

Essentially, mastering the art of retirement planning involves understanding the principles of strategic and cautious investing. Through an extensive understanding of investment fundamentals, careful evaluation of risk tolerance, and the building of a diversified portfolio, individuals can pave the way to financial independence and resilience against inflationary challenges. Instead of falling for the false promise of unlimited wealth, retirees should prioritize the need to increase their savings at a rate that outpaces inflation. This will ensure their financial security and a comfortable retirement.

Chapter 13

Deciphering India's WPI and CPI Data: Insights into Economic Trends and Inflation Dynamics

In the ever-changing world of economic analysis, the Wholesale Price Index (WPI) and Consumer Price Index (CPI) are essential tools that have a profound impact on policy decisions, business strategies, and consumer behaviour. This chapter explores a thorough examination of India's WPI and CPI data, uncovering their intricacies and revealing their significant implications for different participants in the economy.

Understanding WPI and CPI

Both the Wholesale Price Index (WPI) and Consumer Price Index (CPI) are crucial indicators that track price movements and gauge inflationary pressures in an economy. WPI monitors fluctuations in the prices of goods at the wholesale level, while CPI gauges changes in the prices of goods and services consumed by households.

Significance of WPI and CPI

Both WPI and CPI serve as important factors in directing monetary policy decisions, fiscal planning, and business strategies. WPI serves as an important instrument for predicting potential inflationary pressures in the production pipeline, offering valuable insights into cost dynamics for businesses and policymakers. On the other hand, CPI provides a straightforward evaluation of the inflation that households experience, impacting wage discussions, spending habits, and buying ability.

Methodologies of Calculation

Calculating WPI and CPI requires precise methodologies designed to capture price fluctuations across various sectors and categories. WPI gathers price data from wholesale markets, prioritizing production volumes and market significance. Conversely, CPI collects price data from a wide variety of household-use products and services, offering insights into consumer spending patterns and behaviour.

Implications for Stakeholders

The WPI and CPI data carry far-reaching implications for policymakers, businesses, and consumers:

- **Policymakers**: Central banks and government agencies rely on WPI and CPI data to formulate monetary policy, set interest rates, and implement measures to control inflation. The inflation targets set based on CPI data guide policy interventions aimed at maintaining price stability and economic growth.

- **Businesses**: WPI serves as a crucial input for businesses in pricing decisions, production planning, and supply chain management. Fluctuations in WPI influence input costs, profit margins, and pricing strategies across industries, impacting competitiveness and profitability.

- **Consumers**: CPI data directly affect consumers' purchasing power, cost of living, and inflation expectations. Rising CPI may erode real incomes, prompt adjustments in household budgets, and influence consumption patterns, thereby shaping overall economic activity.

Interpreting WPI-CPI Divergence

Both the WPI and CPI track price movements, but they may show different trends because of differences in their coverage, composition, and weighting methods. Variations in the considered basket of goods and services, the handling of indirect taxes, and the timing of price adjustments can lead to discrepancies in inflation rates.

Example: Food Inflation Dynamics

Both the WPI and CPI baskets in India give significant importance to food prices, reflecting their impact on household expenses and overall inflation trends. Changes in food prices, caused by a variety of factors such as weather conditions, supply chain disruptions, and government policies, can lead to differences between WPI and CPI inflation rates.

Essentially, WPI and CPI data are extremely useful tools for tracking price changes, assessing inflationary trends, and guiding decision-making in various economic sectors. Through a deep understanding of these indices and their implications, individuals can confidently navigate the economic landscape, promoting long-term growth and stability.

Chapter 14

Navigating India's Monetary Policy Landscape: Insights into the Role of the RBI and Global Interdependencies

A key component of India's monetary policy framework, the Reserve Bank of India (RBI) has the responsibility of maintaining price stability, promoting economic expansion, and safeguarding financial stability. But the RBI's policy discussions take place in the context of a complicated and interconnected global economy, where the decisions made by big central banks have an international impact on domestic policy decisions and economic results.

Interplay of Global Economic Dynamics

The RBI, which gives special consideration to the actions of prominent central banks like the US Federal Reserve (Fed), tightly connects the global economic dynamics to its policy decisions. The Fed's monetary stimulus plans, interest rate adjustments, and quantitative easing initiatives have a significant impact on international capital flows, currency rates, and financial market conditions. As a result, the RBI is indirectly under pressure to adjust its own policy responses appropriately.

1. The RBI's Mandate and Objectives

The dual objective of ensuring price stability and promoting economic growth is at the core of the RBI's monetary policy framework. The RBI must use a variety of policy tools to manage inflation, support employment, and advance sustainable economic development in order to strike this difficult balance.

Example: Inflation Targeting Framework

In recent years, the RBI has implemented an inflation targeting framework, in which it establishes an inflation goal range and modifies monetary policy tools, including the repo rate, to meet this target. The RBI wants to support macroeconomic stability and boost economic confidence by linking inflation expectations to a stable base and confirming its commitment to price control.

2. Global Interdependencies and Policy Spill overs

The monetary policy decisions made by India are susceptible to the influence of global economic forces, especially those originating from developed economies such as the United States. The US Federal Reserve's initiatives, such as interest rate adjustments and quantitative easing programs, may have a significant impact on India's financial markets and monetary policy position.

Example: Impact of US Fed Policy on Rupee and Capital Flows

Shifts in US monetary policy, such as interest rate hikes or cuts, can impact the rupee's value and local interest rates, and can also influence capital flows into and out of India. Furthermore, the US Federal Reserve's activities may cause changes in global investor mood and risk appetite, which could increase volatility in the Indian financial markets and make it more difficult for the RBI to maintain stability.

3. Policy Coordination and Exchange Rate Management

The RBI must carefully adjust its monetary policy stance to take into account external developments while achieving its domestic goals because of the interconnectedness of the global economy. To reduce volatility and promote trade and investment flows, it is frequently necessary to actively regulate the exchange rate in addition to collaborating with other central banks and governments.

Example: RBI's Forex Interventions

In order to keep the rupee stable and limit excessive volatility, the RBI often intervenes in the foreign exchange market. The Reserve Bank of India (RBI) can influence the exchange rate and lessen economic disruptions caused by sudden changes in currency values by purchasing or disposing of foreign exchange reserves. This helps to maintain investor confidence and external stability.

4. Navigating Uncertainties and Trade-offs

The RBI must overcome significant obstacles to reconcile national interests with international interdependencies, requiring it to make tough trade-offs between conflicting goals. Uncertainties about geopolitical unrest, policy changes in advanced economies, and global economic conditions complicate the RBI's decision-making process.

Example: Managing Inflation-Foreign Exchange Trade-offs

The RBI frequently encounters challenges in simultaneously controlling inflation and exchange rate stability. A declining rupee might worsen inflationary pressures by increasing import costs, but an excessive appreciation can reduce export competitiveness. Achieving equilibrium between these goals needs thoughtful policy interventions and forward-thinking approaches.

5. Forward Guidance and Communication

In order to shape market expectations and affect economic outcomes, the RBI's monetary policy tools must include effective communication and forward guidance. Monetary policy execution is more successful and promotes financial market stability when there is clear and open communication about policy aims, data dependencies, and risk assessments.

Example: RBI's Bi-monthly Monetary Policy Reviews

RBI's bi-monthly monetary policy reviews serve as key communication channels for conveying policy decisions, assessments of economic conditions, and forward guidance to market participants and the public. These reviews provide insights into the RBI's policy stance, inflation forecasts, and growth projections, guiding market expectations and influencing interest rate dynamics.

In conclusion, the Reserve Bank of India (RBI) operates within a dynamic global economic environment where its policy decisions are influenced by both domestic factors and external forces beyond its control. While the RBI maintains autonomy in crafting monetary policies that address India's unique economic challenges, it must also consider the impact of global economic trends, especially those driven by major central banks like the US Federal Reserve.

Despite these external pressures, the RBI remains committed to its mandate of promoting sustainable growth, ensuring price stability, and fostering financial resilience within the Indian economy. By carefully navigating the complexities of global economic dynamics and exercising prudent judgment, the RBI strives to steer the Indian economy towards a path of stability, prosperity, and resilience in the face of global uncertainties.

Chapter 15

Unraveling the Dynamics of Consumer Spending: Fueling Economic Growth

Consumer expenditure generates the demand for products and services, stimulates production, and promotes economic expansion. It is the cornerstone of economic activity. This chapter explores the critical role that consumer spending plays in driving economic growth. It clarifies how every rupee that consumers spend can potentially circulate many times, multiplying its impact and adding to the overall prosperity of the economy.

1. The Engine of Economic Activity

Consumer spending contributes significantly to aggregate demand, influencing the performance of the retail, hotel, healthcare, and leisure sectors of the economy. Businesses adjust by increasing production, creating more jobs, and investing in capacity development to match the rising demand as consumers devote more of their income to consumption.

Example: The Ripple Effect of Dining Out

Let's say a family chooses to eat dinner at a nearby restaurant. They pay for their meals and beverages as they eat, which contributes to the restaurant's revenues. The restaurant uses this revenue to pay for all of its operational expenses, such as rent, utilities, and employee salaries.

Now, let's follow the ripple effect of this transaction:

A. **Restaurant Expenses**: The restaurant uses its revenue to pay various expenses, such as purchasing ingredients from suppliers, paying rent for its space, settling utility bills, and compensating its employees.

B. **Supplier Transactions**: The suppliers who provide ingredients to the restaurant receive payment for their goods. This income enables them to cover their own expenses, such as wages for their employees, transportation costs, and raw material purchases.

C. **Employee Income**: The restaurant employees, including chefs, servers, and cleaners, receive their salaries or wages. They, in turn, use this income to support their livelihoods by paying for housing, groceries, transportation, and other essential expenses.

D. **Grocery Purchases**: Let's focus on the grocery expenses of one of the restaurant's employees. They use part of their income to buy groceries from a local market. The grocery store then earns revenue from these sales, which it uses to pay its own suppliers, cover operational costs, and compensate its employees.

E. **Farmers and Producers**: Finally, the local farmers or producers who supply goods to the grocery store receive payment for their products. This income allows them to invest in their farms, purchase equipment or seeds, and support their families.

This sequence of events demonstrates how a single act of restaurant consumption initiates a number of financial transactions, setting off a cascade effect that fosters economic growth and sustains livelihoods across the community.

2. The Multiplier Effect

The multiplier effect, which measures the economic impact of every rupee spent, is one of the fundamental ideas underpinning consumer purchasing. When consumers spend money, it starts a domino effect that generates more income and spending. Each cycle of spending generates revenue for others, who then spend some of their earnings, amplifying the initial effect.

Example: The Tenfold Multiplier

Let's illustrate the multiplier effect with a hypothetical scenario:

A. **Initial Consumer Spending**: A consumer spends ₹100 on groceries at a local store.

B. **Revenue for the Grocery Store**: The grocery store earns ₹100 in revenue from the sale. It uses a portion of this revenue to cover operating expenses, such as rent, utilities, and employee wages.

C. **Supplier Payments**: The grocery store purchases goods from its suppliers, paying them ₹70 for the products. The suppliers, in turn, use this income to pay their own expenses, such as wages for their employees and raw material purchases.

D. **Employee Income**: Let's assume that the suppliers allocate ₹50 of the payment received from the grocery store to wages for their employees. These employees then have ₹50 in additional income, which they spend on various goods and services.

E. **Secondary Consumer Spending**: The employees spend ₹50 on dining at a local restaurant. The restaurant earns revenue from this expenditure and uses it to cover expenses, pay suppliers, and compensate its employees.

F. **Supplier Transactions and Employee Income**: The restaurant pays its suppliers, who use a portion of this income to pay their employees. The cycle continues as employees spend their wages on goods and services, creating additional income for others in the economy.

G. **Iterative Process**: This cycle of spending and income generation continues, with each round of expenditure contributing to economic activity and income generation. The initial ₹100 spent by the consumer has now circulated through the economy multiple times, generating income for various businesses and individuals along the way.

The multiplier effect provides the possibility for the initial ₹100 in consumer spending to boost economic activity much beyond its original worth, highlighting the critical role that consumer spending plays in promoting prosperity and overall economic growth.

3. Factors Influencing Consumer Spending

Consumer confidence, interest rates, employment prospects, disposable income levels, and inflationary expectations are some of the elements that affect consumer buying patterns. Variations in these factors have the power to influence consumer behaviour, which in turn shapes the state of the economy as a whole by influencing the tendency to spend, save, or invest.

Example: Consumer Confidence

Imagine a situation where robust GDP growth, steady inflation, low unemployment rates, and stable inflation lead to great consumer confidence. In this atmosphere, people are optimistic about their financial futures and the overall status of the economy. They consequently have a greater willingness to spend money on luxuries like technology, trips, and refurbishing their homes.

For example, a family feeling confident about their future and able to afford such purchases might decide to upgrade their kitchen appliances or buy a new car. This increased spending boosts demand throughout the economy, resulting in more corporate sales, higher output, and job creation.

On the other hand, consumer confidence may drastically decline during times of economic uncertainty or recession. For instance, people might start saving and spending more sparingly if they are worried about growing unemployment, inflationary pressures, or geopolitical instability. They could put off big purchases, spend less on frivolous expenditures, and take a more cautious approach to money management.

This drop in consumer spending may affect the economy as a whole, leading to fewer sales for companies, lower production levels, and potentially job losses. Economic growth may decelerate as companies reduce their operations in response to lower demand, worsening the slump and further undermining consumer confidence.

All things considered, consumer confidence is a major factor in determining consumer spending patterns and the general course of the economy. While low confidence might lead to economic contraction or stagnation, high confidence can drive economic expansion. Therefore, companies and policymakers closely monitor consumer sentiment as a crucial indicator of the stability and health of the economy.

4. Policy Implications

To boost economic activity and influence consumer spending habits, policymakers frequently use a variety of initiatives. For instance, central banks can implement monetary policies focused on reducing interest rates in order to boost borrowing and spending during times of economic slowdown or recession.

Fiscal policies can also promote consumer spending on products and services by putting more money in their pockets through initiatives like tax cuts or stimulus packages. Governments can, for instance, give people direct cash transfers or tax rebates to encourage consumption and boost aggregate demand.

Furthermore, by improving household stability and economic prospects, investments in social welfare, infrastructure, and job development programs can indirectly raise consumer confidence. People are more likely to boost discretionary spending and support economic growth when they feel safe in their jobs and financial situations.

Furthermore, legislative changes that encourage fair competition, better consumer protection, and increased market transparency can boost consumer confidence and economic trust. Legislators may promote an atmosphere that encourages consumers to make long-term financial commitments and investments by tackling issues pertaining to fraud, unfair tactics, and market swings.

In order to boost consumer spending, stimulate economic growth, and advance general welfare, authorities must take a multipronged approach that incorporates monetary, fiscal, and regulatory policies. Policymakers could lay the foundation for resilient and sustained economic growth by carefully adjusting policies to reflect consumer moods and current economic realities.

Finally, we should acknowledge that consumer spending plays a significant role in driving economic expansion, creating demand, creating jobs, and fostering social development. Understanding the wide range of consumer expenditures reveals the complex web of economic exchanges that shape our everyday lives, influencing the economy's course and impacting the well-being of its constituents. Let us acknowledge the critical role that consumer purchasing has played in influencing our common path toward sustained growth and shared prosperity as we navigate the intricacies of economic dynamics.

Chapter 16

Navigating the World of Investments: Strategies for Financial Growth

Building wealth, reaching financial objectives, and ensuring long-term success all depend heavily on investing. We set out on a journey through the varied terrain of investments in this chapter, hoping to provide readers with the knowledge and tools they need to manage the complexities of financial markets and make intelligent choices.

1. Understanding Investment Basics

Investing is essentially the process of putting resources, such as cash, time, or effort, into assets in the hope of making a profit or reaching particular financial goals. The world of investment alternatives is wide and diverse, with everything from stocks and bonds to real estate and commodities having a unique risk-return profile and growth potential.

Example: Diversification

Spreading investments over several asset classes, industries, and geographical areas in order to reduce risk and improve portfolio resilience is a basic investing strategy. In order to minimize long-term losses and protect against possible losses, investors might minimize their exposure to any one asset or market area by diversifying their assets.

2. Investment Vehicles and Asset Classes

There are many different asset classes and investment options available to investors, each with its own advantages and disadvantages.

A. **Stocks:** Stocks represent ownership in a company and offer the potential for capital appreciation and dividends. They are traded on stock exchanges and can provide significant returns but also come with higher volatility and risk.

B. **Bonds:** Bonds are debt securities issued by governments, municipalities, or corporations to raise capital. Investors lend money to the issuer in exchange for periodic interest payments and the return of the principal amount at maturity. Bonds are generally considered less risky than stocks but offer lower potential returns.

C. **Mutual Funds:** Mutual funds pool money from multiple investors to invest in a diversified portfolio of stocks, bonds, or other assets. They offer professional management and diversification, making them suitable for investors seeking a hands-off approach to investing.

D. **Exchange-Traded Funds (ETFs):** ETFs are similar to mutual funds but trade on stock exchanges like individual stocks. They offer diversification, liquidity, and low expense ratios, making them popular among investors looking for cost-effective exposure to various market segments.

E. **Real Estate Investment Trusts (REITs):** REITs are companies that own, operate, or finance income-generating real estate properties. They provide investors with exposure to the real estate market and typically offer attractive dividends and potential for capital appreciation.

Prior to selecting asset classes and investment instruments that meet their financial goals, investors should carefully consider their time horizon, risk tolerance, and investing goals. Furthermore, diversification across several asset classes can improve long-term returns and lower overall portfolio risk.

3. Risk Management and Investment Strategies

Successful investing requires both risk management and investment techniques, which call for a disciplined strategy suited to each investor's goals, time horizon, and risk tolerance. Investors can select from a variety of tactics, such as:

A. **Value Investing:** Value investors seek to identify undervalued stocks trading below their intrinsic value. They focus on companies with strong fundamentals, sound management, and favourable long-term prospects, aiming to buy low and sell high.

B. **Growth Investing:** Growth investors target companies with high potential for earnings growth, often in innovative industries or emerging markets. They prioritize companies with strong revenue growth, market leadership, and competitive advantages, aiming to capitalize on future growth prospects.

C. **Income Investing:** Income investors prioritize generating regular income from their investments, typically through dividends, interest payments, or rental income. They focus on assets such as dividend-paying stocks, bonds, and real estate investment trusts (REITs), aiming to build a steady stream of passive income.

D. **Momentum Trading:** Momentum traders seek to capitalize on short-term price trends and market momentum, buying assets that have been performing well and selling those that have been underperforming. They use technical analysis and market indicators to identify trends and execute trades quickly to capture potential profits.

Example: SIP (Systematic Investment Plan)

Regardless of market conditions, SIP (Systematic Investment Plan) is a popular investment technique that entails making regular, fixed-amount investments in a certain asset or fund. An investor might, for instance, put ₹5,000 into a mutual fund each month. This strategy helps lessen market volatility by having the investor purchase more shares or units during periods of low prices and fewer during periods of high prices. SIP (Systematic Investment Plan) offers the potential to improve long-term profits by gradually lowering the average cost per share or unit acquired.

4. Investment Planning and Asset Allocation

Creating a well-diversified portfolio based on each investor's financial objectives, risk tolerance, and investment horizon is essential to effective investment planning. A key component of portfolio creation and optimization is asset allocation, which is the method of allocating investments across various asset classes according to their expected risk and return characteristics.

Example: Retirement Planning

Investors may choose to use a strategic asset allocation method to achieve long-term objectives like retirement, dividing growth-oriented assets like stocks amongst income-producing assets like bonds and fixed-income instruments. Investors can achieve effective risk management and portfolio return optimization by matching assets to specific time horizons and liquidity requirements.

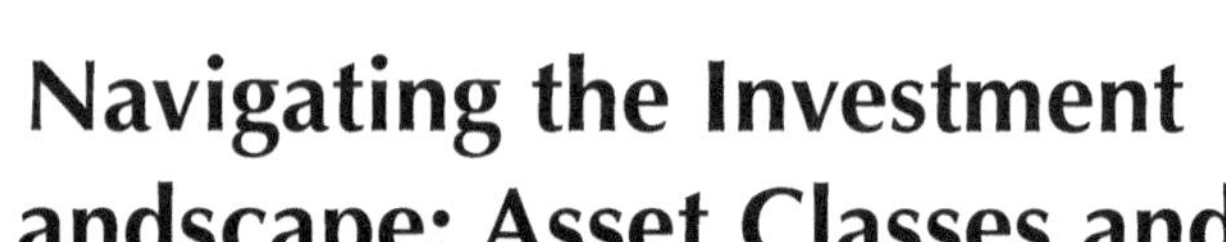

Chapter 17

Navigating the Investment Landscape: Asset Classes and Diversification Strategies

Let's analyse successful diversification tactics and explore the wide range of asset classes. Investors can reduce risk and improve portfolio resilience by distributing their assets among a variety of asset classes, each of which provides distinct qualities and potential returns. Now let's take a closer look at each asset class and talk about the best diversification tactics.

1 – Fixed Deposits

Now let's talk about emergency funds and diversification in relation to fixed deposits (FDs). You recognize the value of fixed deposits in diversifying investment portfolios and providing a dependable source of emergency funds, even though you may not believe in them because they cannot outperform inflation. Because fixed deposits yield a steady and predictable return, they're a good option for capital preservation and emergency liquidity. When combined with other diverse investments, fixed deposits help reduce total risk and guarantee cash on hand for unforeseen expenses.

The best times for fixed deposits are when the economy is experiencing high interest rates, fixed deposits are best. Individuals can optimize fixed deposit returns during periods of high interest rates. Rising interest rates result in higher yields on fixed deposits, which improves the possibility of generating income and protecting wealth. Consequently, investors may want to think about putting money into fixed deposits at these times in order to take advantage of beneficial interest rate settings. This tactical approach can improve portfolio performance overall and maximize profits. Let's now talk about additional asset classes and the advantages of diversification.

Pitfalls to Avoid with Fixed Deposits

When it comes to fixed deposits, it's important to be cautious and steer clear of certain risks. The following are important things to remember:

- **Overallocation of Funds:** One should never allocate more funds to fixed deposits than necessary for emergency funds or as a small portion of overall asset diversification.

- **Tax Implications:** Consider the impact of taxes on fixed deposit returns, especially if you fall into a higher tax bracket. Individuals in the highest tax bracket may incur significant tax liabilities on the interest earned from fixed deposits.

- **Inflationary Erosion:** Even if a fixed deposit offers a relatively high interest rate, the after-tax return may not be sufficient to outpace the prevailing inflation rate. Inflation typically ranges from 4% to 7%, and if the after-tax return fails to exceed this rate, the real value of the investment will diminish over time.

For example, if a person is in the highest tax band (30%) and the fixed deposit rates vary from 4% to 8% based on tenure, they should carefully review the after-tax returns to make sure they sufficiently offset inflationary pressures.

Investors may make educated judgments regarding their fixed deposit investments and make sure they are in line with their overall financial objectives and risk tolerance by being aware of these hazards, taking into account the individual fixed deposit rates, and examining the tax consequences. Let us now examine additional asset types and the factors that affect their diversification.

2 – GOLD

When it comes to asset diversification, gold is a classic and priceless addition to any well-diversified investing portfolio. Gold has attracted investors for ages due to its intrinsic value, stability, and hedging capabilities. It provides a dependable hedge against market volatility and economic concerns. This chapter introduces us to a thorough examination of gold as an asset class, explaining its special qualities, historical relevance, and function in diversification plans.

A. Gold's Everlasting Appeal

Gold's appeal cuts across decades and cultural boundaries because it embodies both material wealth and metaphorical meaning. Due to its rarity, strength, and aesthetic appeal, people have treasured gold as a store of value and a symbol of affluence throughout human history. Gold's appeal has persisted throughout history, from prehistoric societies to contemporary economies, acting as a reliable medium of exchange and a physical asset during uncertain economic times.

B. The Hedge Against Uncertainty

Gold appears as a reliable hedge against uncertainty in an era characterized by global tensions, economic upheavals, and financial market volatility. Unlike conventional assets like equities and bonds, gold remains unaffected by market fluctuations or economic cycles, maintaining its intrinsic value and purchasing power over time. Gold frequently has negative associations with other financial instruments due to its lack of correlation, which helps with portfolio volatility in choppy market conditions and promotes diversification.

C. Diversification Benefits of Gold

Including gold in an investment portfolio protects its overall performance by increasing diversification and reducing risk. Gold's value either stays relatively steady or increases during times of market hardship due to its poor connection with traditional assets like bonds and stocks. The benefit of diversity is most noticeable when there is a currency depreciation, a geopolitical crisis, or an economic slump because gold is a solid safe haven asset.

D. Practical Considerations for Gold Investment

You can purchase gold in a variety of ways, such as coins, real bullion, exchange-traded funds (ETFs), and stock in gold mining companies. Every investment vehicle offers different advantages and considerations based on investors' preferences, risk tolerance, and investment goals. In addition, one should carefully evaluate taxation, liquidity, and storage costs prior to adding gold to an investment portfolio.

E. Conclusion: Embracing Gold in Diversification Strategies

To sum up, gold holds a pivotal role in the domain of asset diversification due to its unmatched stability, hedging capabilities, and inherent worth. Investors can increase portfolio diversification, reduce risk, and safeguard wealth in a variety of market scenarios by adding gold. For prudent investors looking to strengthen their financial stability and accomplish long-term wealth preservation, gold continues to be an essential asset. You can use it as a hedge against inflation, a refuge in times of crisis, or a symbol of perpetual prosperity.

F. Cons of Physical Gold

- **Storage and Security Concerns:** Storing physical gold entails costs and security concerns, as investors need secure facilities or safe deposit boxes to safeguard their holdings from theft or loss. These storage costs can erode returns over time and add complexity to managing physical gold investments.

- **Transaction Costs:** Buying and selling physical gold may involve transaction costs, including dealer premiums, assay fees, and transportation expenses. These costs can reduce overall returns and liquidity, particularly for small-scale investors or those dealing with small quantities of gold.

- **Limited Income Potential:** Unlike financial assets such as stocks or bonds, physical gold does not generate income in the form of dividends or interest payments. Investors rely solely on capital appreciation for returns, which may be limited compared to income-generating investments over the long term.

Sovereign Gold Bonds (SGB): A Superior Alternative to Physical Gold

Sovereign Gold Bonds (SGBs) are an attractive investment option that have gained significant popularity. They have several advantages over traditional physical gold ownership. When we examine the differences between SGBs and real gold, it is clear that SGBs offer investors a number of convincing reasons for why they are a better option. Let's take a closer look at these causes:

A. Convenience and Safety

The ease of use and security that SGBs provide over real gold is one of their main advantages. SGBs are held electronically, so there is no need for physical storage and the related security risks that come with it. This is in contrast to actual gold, which needs safe storage arrangements and insurance against loss or theft. Through demat accounts, investors may easily transact and maintain their SGB holdings, offering a hassle-free and secure investing experience.

B. Fixed Interest Income

SGBs give investors the chance to benefit from both prospective capital growth and fixed interest income, in contrast to actual gold, which has no income. The Government of India consistently provides investors with an income stream over the bond's duration, crediting interest on SGBs every six months. For investors who prioritize their income, SGB investments are a desirable choice because of the fixed interest income that increases their overall returns.

C. Tax Efficiency

Compared to real gold, SGBs are taxed more favourably, providing advantages on both interest income and capital gains. While capital gains from the redemption or sale of SGBs are tax-free if held until maturity, interest received on SGBs is taxable at the investor's income tax slab rate. For investors who are concerned about taxes, the tax-efficient structure of SGB investments improves the after-tax profits.

D. Liquidity and Tradability

Due to their high liquidity and tradability, SGBs enable investors to transact on secondary markets or on stock exchanges by buying, selling, or transferring their bonds. Because of this liquidity feature, investors can manage their investment portfolios with more agility and flexibility, taking advantage of opportunities in the market or modifying their asset mix to meet their investment goals.

E. Capital Protection and Sovereign Guarantee

SGBs provide investors with a state guarantee and capital protection as sovereign-backed instruments, reducing counterparty risk and increasing overall investment security. Investors can feel confident in the investment product because the Government of India stands behind SGB issuances, promising to pay interest and redemption proceeds on time.

3 – Government bonds and Public Provident Fund (PPF)

In India, two well-liked investment options are public provident funds (PPF) and government bonds. Both provide investors with a number of advantages, such as stability, safety, and lucrative returns. Here we explore the unique benefits of these investing options and explain why many people view them as the cornerstones of their financial planning.

A. Government Bonds

- **Safety and Security:** Government bonds, issued by the Government of India, are considered one of the safest investment options available to investors. Backed by the sovereign guarantee, these bonds offer unparalleled safety of principal, ensuring that investors' capital is protected against default risk.

- **Stable Returns:** Government bonds provide investors with stable and predictable returns through periodic interest payments, typically semi-annually or annually. The fixed interest payments offer a reliable source of income, making government bonds particularly attractive for income-oriented investors seeking steady cash flows.

- **Diversification Benefits:** Government bonds serve as an effective diversification tool within an investment portfolio, helping investors spread risk and reduce overall portfolio volatility. By adding government bonds to their investment mix, investors can achieve greater stability and resilience against market fluctuations.

- **Tax Efficiency:** Certain categories of government bonds, such as tax-free bonds and sovereign gold bonds, offer tax advantages to investors. Interest income earned from tax-free bonds is exempt from income tax, while capital gains arising from sovereign gold bonds are tax-exempt if held until maturity. This tax-efficient structure enhances the after-tax returns from government bonds, making them an attractive option for tax-conscious investors.

B. Public Provident Fund (PPF)

- **Long-Term Wealth Accumulation:** PPF is a long-term savings instrument designed to help individuals build a retirement corpus and achieve long-term financial goals. With a tenure of 15 years, PPF encourages disciplined savings habits and fosters wealth accumulation over the long term.

- **Tax-Free Returns:** The returns generated from PPF investments are tax-free, offering investors the opportunity to enjoy compounded growth without any tax liability. Additionally, contributions made to PPF qualify for tax deductions under Section 80C of the Income Tax Act, further enhancing the tax benefits associated with PPF investments.

- **Flexibility and Liquidity:** While PPF has a lock-in period of 15 years, it offers partial withdrawal facilities from the seventh year onwards, providing investors with liquidity and flexibility in managing their financial needs. The ability to make partial withdrawals ensures that investors can access their funds in times of emergencies without compromising the long-term objectives of the investment.

- **Power of Compounding:** One of the most potent features of PPF is the power of compounding, which allows investors to generate substantial wealth over time through the reinvestment of interest income. As interest compounds annually, even small regular contributions can grow into a significant corpus over the long term, making PPF an invaluable tool for wealth creation.

- **Sovereign Backing:** PPF is backed by the Government of India, providing investors with the assurance of capital protection and sovereign guarantee. The government's backing instills confidence and trust in the investment product, making PPF a preferred choice for risk-averse investors seeking stability and security.

4 – Equity Investments

Investments in equity provide investors with ownership stakes in companies and the chance to take part in their expansion and financial success. Investors who buy shares in publicly listed corporations become shareholders, entitled to a share of the earnings and possibly an increase in the value of their investments. Here, we will understand the complexities of equity investments, highlighting their attributes, advantages, and investor considerations.

A. Understanding Equity Investments

Purchasing shares or stocks of publicly traded corporations grants investors ownership rights as well as a claim on the business's profits and assets. Equities have a bigger potential return than fixed-income investments like bonds, but they also carry a higher level of risk and volatility.

B. Benefits of Equity Investments

- **Potential for High Returns:** Historically, equities have delivered higher returns than most other asset classes over the long term, making them a cornerstone of wealth creation and capital appreciation.

- **Ownership and Control:** Equity investors hold ownership stakes in companies, granting them voting rights and a say in corporate decisions through annual general meetings and proxy voting.

- **Portfolio Diversification:** Including equities in an investment portfolio can diversify risk and enhance overall portfolio performance, as stocks often have low correlation with other asset classes such as bonds and real estate.

- **Liquidity:** Stocks trade on public exchanges, providing investors with liquidity and the ability to buy or sell shares quickly and easily, enhancing flexibility and market access.

C. Considerations for Equity Investments

- **Risk and Volatility:** Equities are subject to market volatility and price fluctuations, influenced by factors such as economic conditions, company performance, and investor sentiment. Investors must be prepared to withstand short-term fluctuations for long-term wealth accumulation.

- **Research and Due Diligence:** Successful equity investing requires thorough research and analysis of companies, industries, and market trends. Investors should assess factors such as financial performance, competitive positioning, and growth prospects before making investment decisions.

- **Diversification:** Diversifying across sectors, industries, and geographic regions can mitigate risk and enhance portfolio resilience. A well-diversified equity portfolio spreads risk and reduces the impact of individual stock performance on overall returns.

- **Investment Horizon:** Equity investments are best suited for long-term investors with a horizon of five years or more. Timing the market or engaging in short-term trading can be speculative and may lead to suboptimal returns.

D. Strategies for Equity Investments

- **Value Investing:** Value investors seek undervalued stocks trading below their intrinsic value, aiming to capitalize on potential price appreciation as the market corrects its valuation discrepancies.

- **Growth Investing:** Growth investors focus on companies with strong growth potential, prioritizing revenue and earnings growth over current profitability. These stocks often trade at higher valuations but offer the prospect of significant long-term gains.

- **Dividend Investing:** Dividend investors target companies with a track record of consistent dividend payments and dividend growth. Dividend-paying stocks provide regular income streams and can be attractive for income-oriented investors seeking steady cash flows.

5. Mastering Equity Investing

Making wise investment selections in the world of stock investing requires a grasp of the subtle differences between various company and industry types. Every category, from agile small-cap businesses to massive large-cap companies, presents different opportunities and difficulties. We explore the dynamics of large-cap, mid-cap, and small-cap companies, analyse sectoral growth prospects, solve the puzzles of balance sheet analysis, and more as we delve deeper into the complexities of stock investing on this topic.

A. Large-Cap Companies

Large-cap businesses, known by many as "blue-chip stocks," are well-established market leaders with substantial market valuations. Usually, these industry veterans have long operating histories, well-established brand identities, and steady revenue streams. Large-cap firms are popular among conservative investors looking for consistent returns with less volatility because they provide stability, liquidity, and possible dividends.

B. Mid-Cap Companies

Offering a balance of risk and growth potential, mid-cap companies fall between large-cap behemoths and small-cap start-ups. These businesses have the potential for rapid growth and market outperformance, as well as modest market capitalisations. Mid-cap companies can expose investors to new growth prospects and innovation inside their particular industry, but they do demand a higher volatility tolerance.

C. Small-Cap Companies

Small-cap firms, which include high-growth businesses with low market capitalizations and nascent startups, embody the market's entrepreneurial spirit. Due to their relative lack of financial resources and market awareness, small-cap companies are riskier, but they also present a chance for enormous gains and exponential growth. Small-cap stocks can experience substantial market changes and volatility, so investing in them calls for careful consideration, perseverance, and a lengthy investment horizon.

D. Sectoral Analysis and Growth Prospects

Promising investment opportunities require an understanding of sectoral dynamics and development potential. The potential for growth, cyclicality, and vulnerability to macroeconomic conditions varies throughout industries. To identify sectors poised for growth and innovation, sectoral analysis entails evaluating competitive landscapes, industry trends, regulatory contexts, and technological advancements.

E. Balance Sheet Analysis

An essential component of stock research is analysing a company's balance sheet, which offers information about its solvency, liquidity, and overall financial health. Essential measurements, including the debt-to-equity ratio, return on equity, and current ratio, provide insightful insights into the financial health and operational effectiveness of a business. Investors closely examine balance sheets in order to analyse risk, assess management's capital allocation choices, and determine the company's resilience to economic downturns and growth opportunities.

"If navigating the complexities of individual stock selection seems daunting, mutual funds offer a professionally managed alternative suited to your investment needs."

6 – Mutual Funds

Mutual funds are collective investment vehicles that combine the funds of several individuals to make diversified stock, bond, or other security investments. Professionally run, mutual funds provide investors with access to a broad spectrum of asset classes, investment approaches, and risk profiles. This topic provides an in-depth discussion of mutual fund characteristics, advantages, and investment considerations.

Types of Mutual Funds

- **Equity Funds:** These funds invest primarily in stocks, offering growth potential over the long term. They are further categorized based on market capitalization, including large-cap, mid-cap, and small-cap funds, catering to investors' risk tolerance and investment objectives.

- **Debt Funds:** Debt funds invest in fixed-income securities such as bonds and government securities, offering steady income and capital preservation. They are suitable for conservative investors seeking stable returns and lower volatility.

- **Hybrid Funds:** Hybrid funds invest in a mix of equities and debt instruments, offering a balanced approach to portfolio diversification and risk management. They cater to investors seeking a blend of growth and income with moderate risk.

- **Sectoral Funds:** Sectoral funds focus on specific sectors or industries such as technology, healthcare, or banking, providing targeted exposure to thematic investment themes. They are suitable for investors bullish on particular sectors or seeking sector-specific diversification.

A. Risk Management and Diversification

A multiplier is one of the main benefits of mutual funds. Mutual funds distribute risk and lessen the effect of a single stock's performance on the portfolio's total returns by investing in a variety of securities across many asset classes, industries, and geographic areas. Diversification lowers risk and volatility, hence enhancing portfolio stability and resilience in changing market conditions.

B. Professional Management

Experienced fund managers oversee mutual funds, manage portfolios, and do research and analysis on behalf of investors. To optimize returns while controlling risk, these experts use a range of investment methods and approaches. In order to make well-informed investment decisions and maximize portfolio performance, fund managers constantly track market movements, economic indicators, and stock valuations.

C. Variety of Investment Options

There are several investment choices available through mutual funds that suit various time horizons, risk tolerances, and financial goals. Investors have a variety of mutual fund types and strategies to pick from, from fixed-income funds offering steady income streams to equity funds aiming for growth. In order to offer a balanced method of portfolio building, hybrid funds also mix equities and bonds.

D. Convenience and Accessibility

Investors of all experience and financial levels can easily and affordably invest in mutual funds. Without requiring a tremendous deal of study or careful selection of individual securities, mutual funds provide investors with access to competent management and diversity. Mutual funds provide simplicity and flexibility in investment, with minimal minimum commitment requirements and the option to invest through systematic investment plans (SIPs).

E. Transparency and Regulation

Because mutual funds are subject to transparency and regulatory control, investors can obtain detailed information on their holdings, performance, and costs. Regulatory agencies such as the Securities and Exchange Board of India (SEBI) ensure adherence to disclosure standards, investor protection protocols, and industry best practices, thereby enhancing the trustworthiness of mutual fund investing.

F. Considerations for Investors

- **Investment Objectives:** Investors should align their investment objectives, risk tolerance, and time horizon with the appropriate mutual fund category and strategy.

- **Costs and Expenses:** Mutual funds charge management fees, operating expenses, and other fees, which can impact overall returns. Investors should evaluate fund expenses and fees to assess their impact on investment performance.

- **Past Performance:** While past performance is not indicative of future results, investors may consider historical fund performance as part of their investment decision-making process.

- **Tax Implications:** Mutual fund investments may have tax implications such as capital gains taxes on redemption and dividend distribution taxes. Investors should consider tax efficiency when selecting mutual funds.

Chapter 18

Property Investment: A Contra View

I challenge the conventional knowledge surrounding real estate as an investment instrument because I hold a different perspective in a world where investing in real estate is frequently hailed as a certain way to accumulate wealth and financial security. This chapter will scrutinize the intricacies of real estate investing with a critical eye, emphasizing concealed expenses, often overlooked drawbacks, and alternative methods of investing.

1. The Illusion of Safety

Contrary to popular belief, real estate investing is not immune to market volatility or economic downturns. Real estate is a valuable and dependable asset, but because of changing market conditions, government rules, and demography, its value is highly variable. Investors sometimes ignore the risks involved in real estate investing because they think it is a guaranteed method to preserve wealth.

2. Illiquidity and Inflexibility

Real estate investments are by nature inflexible and illiquid, unlike stocks, bonds, or mutual funds. Selling a house may be an expensive and time-consuming process that includes a lot of paperwork, legal steps, and possible transaction costs. Real estate investments also restrict investors' capacity to adjust to shifting market conditions or take advantage of new trends by tying up funds that could be used in more liquid and dynamic investment options.

3. Hidden Costs and Maintenance Burdens

The many unstated expenses and continuous maintenance requirements that come with owning a property might eventually reduce investment returns. The total cost of owning a home goes well beyond the original purchase price and includes things like property taxes, insurance premiums, maintenance expenditures, and repair costs. Investors sometimes underestimate the financial and operational difficulties involved in tenant management, repairs, and property upkeep, leading to unanticipated costs and decreased profitability.

4. Market Dependency and Location Risks

Economic trends, geography considerations, and local market dynamics all have a significant impact on how well real estate investments succeed. Exposure to location-specific hazards, like oversupply, development, infrastructural developments, and regulatory changes, increases the risk of investing in real estate and can affect rental yields and property values. Furthermore, the cyclical ups and downs of the property market may jeopardize investors' long-term goals of accumulating wealth.

5. Alternative Investment Strategies

Investors should consider other investment options that offer greater growth potential, liquidity, and diversification than relying just on real estate to build wealth. By carefully distributing assets among themselves and among equities, bonds, mutual funds, exchange-traded funds (ETFs), and alternative assets like precious metals, a well-rounded investment portfolio can provide exposure to a range of asset classes and lower risk.

Particularly in India's metro cities, where prices have soared to previously unheard-of heights, several segments of the Indian real estate market have stagnated recently. In view of the apparent increase in property values, the sustainability of future appreciation and the viability of real estate investment as a wealth-building strategy have drawn criticism. Let us examine aspects of the contrarian viewpoint on the Indian real estate market and conventional knowledge about property investment.

A. Stagnant Market Dynamics

Despite high hopes, the Indian real estate industry has shown indications of stagnation recently, with weak demand, excess supply in some areas, and a lethargic investor mood. Developers have found it difficult to clear their current inventory, which has resulted in an accumulation of unsold units and pressure on prices. This stagnation highlights the inherent dangers and unknowns of real estate investing in a market that is becoming more and more unstable.

B. Skyrocketing Prices in Metro Cities

Investor speculation and speculative frenzy have caused recent, explosive increases in metro city real estate values, but their unsustainable growth trajectory has raised concerns about these investments' long-term sustainability. Investors may face severe negative risks during a market correction or economic downturn, as the mismatch between property prices and underlying fundamentals, affordability concerns, and declining rental returns create a perilous situation.

C. Uncertain Future Appreciation

Given the prevailing economic conditions and regulatory obstacles, it is not clear that property prices will appreciate in the future. Traditional market dynamics may be upset, making conventional investment techniques outdated. Examples of these factors include shifting customer tastes, altering metropolitan environments, and technological breakthroughs in the real estate business. As a result, given the inherent dangers and uncertainties in the market, investors should proceed with caution and complete due diligence prior to investing funds in real estate.

D. Mathematical Realities of Property Investment

The prevalent thinking around real estate investing does not necessarily line up with empirical data or sound financial theories from a quantitative perspective. The significant up-front expenditures of purchasing real estate, such as stamp duty, registration fees, and maintenance charges, can have a big effect on the total return on investment. Furthermore, one must consider the opportunity cost of locking up cash in illiquid assets like real estate in comparison to other investment options that provide higher liquidity, diversity, and growth potential.

6. Buying vs Renting a House: A Comprehensive Analysis

One of the biggest financial decisions a person will make in their lifetime is whether to buy or rent a home. Each option has advantages and disadvantages, and the best decision depends on a number of parameters, such as long-term objectives, lifestyle preferences, and financial situation. Let's take a closer look at the advantages and disadvantages of owning vs. renting a home.

A. Financial Considerations

Buying a House

- **Pros**

    - Equity Building: Those who own a home might accumulate equity over time by paying off their loan.

    - Potential for Appreciation: In the long run, real estate can increase in value and act as a hedge against inflation.

    - Tax Benefits: Homeowners may be eligible for property tax deductions and loan interest deductions, lowering their total tax obligation.

- **Cons**

    - High Upfront Costs: Purchasing a home requires a significant upfront investment in addition to the down payment, closing costs, and other fees.

    - Maintenance Expenses: Homeowners are responsible for ongoing maintenance and repairs, which can be costly over time.

- Illiquidity: Real estate is an illiquid asset, meaning it may take time to sell the property and access the equity.

Renting a House

- **Pros**

  - Flexibility: Renting provides more freedom, making it easier for people to move about without having to worry about selling their home.

  - Lower Upfront Costs: Generally, renting involves no down payment costs and a reduced initial outlay of funds.

  - Minimal Maintenance: Maintenance and repairs are the responsibility of the landlord, not the tenant.

- **Cons**

  - No Equity Building: Tenants risk missing out on future appreciation and do not accumulate equity in the property.

  - Rent Increases: Over time, rent prices can rise faster than inflation and make housing more unaffordable.

  - Limited Control: Tenants are not allowed to make significant changes or renovations to the property.

B. Lifestyle Considerations

Buying a House

- **Stability:** Homeownership provides stability and a sense of permanence, allowing individuals to establish roots in a community.

- **Customization:** Homeowners have the freedom to customize and personalize their living space according to their preferences.

Renting a House

- **Flexibility:** Renting offers greater flexibility, allowing individuals to explore different neighbourhood's and living arrangements without long-term commitments.

- **Minimal Responsibilities:** Renters have fewer responsibilities compared to homeowners, with the landlord handling major repairs and maintenance issues.

C. Market Conditions

Buying a House

- Favourable Market Conditions: Purchasing might be more profitable in a buyer's market with low loan rates and reasonably priced homes.

- Long-Term Investment: Purchasing a home is frequently viewed as a long-term investment, with the potential for significant returns over time.

Renting a House

- **High Housing Costs:** In markets where housing costs are high and affordability is limited, renting might be a wiser financial move.

- **Short-Term Flexibility:** Without being constrained by a loan, renting enables people to adjust to shifting market conditions and economic concerns.

Let's examine the differing housing approaches used by Ajinkya and Sujit, two people negotiating Mumbai's complicated real estate market. Their different perspectives on renting versus owning a property uncover enlightening financial ramifications and highlight the complex mechanics of the housing market.

Here's a detailed breakdown of Ajinkya and Sujit's housing scenarios:

Our goal is to refute the myth that long-term property appreciation is always better than stock market investments. Contrary to popular opinion, which holds that holding onto property for long periods of time invariably results in substantial wealth accumulation, we analyse the underlying dynamics and draw comparisons with stock market investing strategies.

Ajinkya's Scenario (Buying a Property)

Loan Details

- **Loan Amount (Principal):** ₹80,00,000

- **Interest Rate:** 8%

- **Loan Tenure:** 20 years

- **Down Payment:** ₹20,00,000

- **House Appreciation:** 6% annually

Calculations

- **Monthly EMI Calculation**

  - Principal (P): ₹80,00,000

  - Monthly Interest Rate (R): 8% annually or 0.6667% monthly (8/12/100)

  - Number of Monthly Payments (N): 20 years × 12 months = 240

  - Monthly EMI: ₹66,915

- **Total Payment Over 20 Years**

  - Total EMI Payment: ₹66,915 × 240 = ₹1,60,59,600

  - Total House Cost (Including Down payment): ₹1,60,59,600 + ₹20,00,000 = ₹1,80,59,600

- **Future Value of the House After 20 Years**

  - Initial Value: ₹1,00,00,000

  - Appreciation: 6% per year compounded

  - Future Value: ₹3,20,71,355

- **Real Gain**

  - Real Gain = Future Value of the House – Total House Cost

  - Real Gain = ₹3,20,71,355 – ₹1,80,59,600 = ₹1,40,11,755

Sujit's Scenario (Renting a Property)

Rent Details

- **Monthly Rent:** ₹30,000

- **Annual Increase in Rent:** 5%

- **Deposit Paid to Landlord:** ₹1,80,000

- **Investment Return:** 12%

Calculations

- **Total Rent Paid Over 20 Years**

  - Initial Annual Rent: ₹30,000 × 12 = ₹3,60,000

  - Rent increases annually by 5%

- First Year Rent: ₹3,60,000

- 20th Year Rent: ₹9,09,691 (5% compounding value)

- Total Rent paid over 20 Years: = ₹1,19,03,068

- Note: Decimal values have been disregarded to facilitate a straightforward calculation for a 5% rent increase.

- **Investment Growth Calculations**

  - Initial Investment: ₹20,00,000 (downpayment)

  - Annual Investment from Savings (difference between EMI and rent)

  - Year 1 Savings: ₹66,915 × 12 − ₹3,60,000 = ₹4,42,980

  - Annual Savings grow as rent increases.

  - Using Future Value of a Series formula for an investment growing at 12%

  - Future Value of ₹20,00,000 at 12% for 20 years: FV = ₹1,92,89,008

  - FV of Annual Investments: More complex, but calculated as a sum of geometric series for each year's investment.

- **Approximate Total Future Value of Investments**

  - Assuming annual investments average around ₹4,42,980 with a 12% return:

  - Average Investment Over 20 Years: ₹4,42,980 × 20 = ₹88,59,600

  - Future Value of Investment Growth:

  - Approx. FV considering compounding effect: More detailed calculation needed but estimate around ₹3,68,83,545

- **Real Gain**

  - Real Gain = Future Value of Investment − Total Rent Paid

  - Real Gain = ₹3,68,83,545 − ₹1,19,39,068 = ₹2,49,44,477

Important Notice: All calculations provided are for illustrative purposes and to explain the concept. Actual results may vary depending on real-life scenarios and specific financial conditions.

Conclusion

Comparing the real gains from both scenarios:

- **Ajinkya's Real Gain:** ₹1,40,11,755

- **Sujit's Real Gain:** ₹2,49,44,477

Over a 20-year period, Sujit's rental and investment plan regularly surpasses Ajinkya's real estate purchases in terms of wealth accumulation. This indicates the possible advantages of investing in a variety of markets rather than depending just on real estate growth.

Unpacking the Myth

The widely held belief is that enormous wealth creation is a natural outcome of long-term property ownership. Supporters of this viewpoint frequently cite historical data that demonstrates how property values have increased over decades, which appears to validate the buy-and-hold investment strategy. But this viewpoint ignores important details and doesn't take other investing options into account.

Flaws in the Argument

An oversimplification of investment ideas is the fault in the equation that links improved wealth development with long-term property appreciation. Although it is true that property values can increase over long periods of time, blaming this only on the length of ownership misses the essential factors that contribute to value building. Additionally, because stock market investors typically employ different tactics and have different expectations, the comparison to stock market investments is sometimes biased.

When it comes to stocks, investors can choose which shares to buy and sell, giving them the opportunity to profit from market fluctuations and book profits. Similar to selling certain firm shares while hanging onto others in their portfolio, this strategy entails selling a portion of their stock holdings while maintaining the remainder.

When investing in real estate, however, it is unrealistic and impossible to sell certain rooms or portions of a property, like the kitchen or drawing room, after a set amount of time. Properties, in contrast to stocks, are indivisible assets for which it is not practical or profitable to sell separate parts.

CREDITS

Author: VRIDHAM

Editor: ARIHANT SHARMA

www.ingramcontent.com/pod-product-compliance
Lightning Source LLC
Chambersburg PA
CBHW041920130726
48007CB00014B/107